• •

"This new series is designed to teach outdoor skills to women in the way they learn. . . . Women of all ages describe how they overcame obstacles, what they enjoyed most, or just how they felt about undertaking a new activity . . . extremely well done and appealing."

—*Library Journal* (starred review)

• •

A Ragged Mountain Press
WOMAN'S GUIDE

 FLY FISHING

A Ragged Mountain Press
WOMAN'S GUIDE

FLY · FISHING

DANA RIKIMARU

Series Editor, Molly Mulhern Gross

RAGGED MOUNTAIN PRESS / McGRAW-HILL

Camden, Maine • New York • San Francisco • Washington, D.C. • Auckland • Bogotá
Caracas • Lisbon • London • Madrid • Mexico City • Milan • Montreal
New Delhi • San Juan • Singapore • Sydney • Tokyo • Toronto

Look for these other Ragged Mountain Press Woman's Guides

Backpacking, Adrienne Hall
Canoeing, Laurie Gullion
Climbing, Shelley Presson
Mountaineering, Andrea Gabbard
Powerboating, Sandy Lindsey
Sailing, Doris Colgate

Scuba Diving, Claire Walters
Sea Kayaking, Shelley Johnson
Skiing, Maggie Loring
Snowboarding, Julia Carlson
Winter Sports, Iseult Devlin

• •

Ragged Mountain Press

A Division of The McGraw-Hill Companies

10 9 8 7 6 5

Library of Congress Cataloging-in-Publication Data
Rikimaru, Dana.
   Fly fishing / Dana Rikimaru.
        p. 2 cm. — (A Ragged Mountain Press woman's guide)
   Includes bibliographical references.
   ISBN 0-07-158185-5 (alk. paper)
   1. Fly fishing. 2. Fly fishing for women. I. Title.
II. Series.
SH456.R556 1999
799.1'24'082—dc21   99-32464
                                        CIP

Questions regarding the content of this book
should be addressed to
   Ragged Mountain Press
   P.O. Box 220, Camden, ME 04843
   http://www.raggedmountainpress.com

Questions regarding the ordering of this book
should be addressed to
   The McGraw-Hill Companies
   Customer Service Department
   P.O. Box 547, Blacklick, OH 43004
   Retail customers: 1-800-262-4729
   Bookstores: 1-800-722-4726

Printed by Quebecor Printing Company, Fairfield, PA
Edited by Patricia Sterling and D. A. Oliver
Design by Carol Inouye, Inkstone Communications Design
Project management by Janet Robbins
Page layout by Shannon Thomas
Illustrations by Elayne Sears

Photographs by Gil Alfring unless otherwise noted: pages 59, 135, courtesy the author; pages 17, 21, 131 courtesy of Reel Women Outfitters; page 18, courtesy Nathan Bilow; pages 45 (top) and 91, courtesy Cheyenne Rouse Photography; page 15, courtesy Tony Demin/Adventure Photo; page 63, courtesy Peter Dennen/Outside Images; page 30, courtesy Michael DeYoung; page 119, courtesy Mark Doolittle/Outside Images; pages 128 and 147, courtesy Ken Graham Agency; pages 36 (bottom), 37–38, 45 (inset), 46, 76, 81 (top), 83, courtesy B. J. Lester; pages 66, 97 (bottom), 107 (bottom), and 108, courtesy Orvis; page 137, courtesy Tony Stone Images; and page 22, courtesy Dennis Welsh.

Band-Aid, Capilene, Dacron, Gore-Tex, Neosporin, Pac-Man, Reel Women Outfitters, Space blanket, Tabasco, and Velcro are registered trademarks.

•••••••••••••••••••••••••••••••••••••

DEDICATION

To all those who have taught me
to love and respect the outdoors
and all nature's creatures.

•••••••••••••••••••••••••••••••••••••

• •

"If you want to have a state of meditation where your mind concentrates only on the experience at hand, you will find it standing in the middle of a beautiful river with a fly rod in your hand."

—Glenda Smith, age 51

• •

Foreword

My first fly-fishing adventure began on my porch, where I struggled to thread a pesky, flimsy fly line up through the eyes on my new fly rod. At 38 years old and the mother of two budding anglers, you'd have thought I'd have a clue about this important skill, or that my husband might have pitched in—but he's not an angler, at least not yet. The balky fly rod kept slipping off my lap as I tried to corral it and reach all the way up its nine-foot length. Finally successful at loading the rod with line (or so I thought), I ambled across the yard to a tree-free area to attempt those graceful casts I'd seen in a recent popular movie. I couldn't understand why flailing the rod forward and back didn't send the line whipping gracefully past my ear to that imaginary trout pool next to the oak tree. Eventually I began to wonder how in the world to propel anything as light as a fly line in the direction of my choosing. It struck me that my endeavor was a bit like trying to push a rope. Determined to make a success of my dry-land fishing, I decided to tie a stick to the line in the hope of improving my odds. Still no luck. Each cast ended with either a spaghetti-like pile of line somewhere in the vicinity of my feet, or a tangle of line wrapped, twig and all, around the end of my rod. Frustrated beyond belief, I packed away the rod for the day when I could corner some knowledgeable fly fisher with my questions.

Eventually I convinced a colleague to help me with my casting. In a matter of days I figured out two things: the first eye on my fly rod wasn't for threading the line through (it's actually called the hook keeper, and is meant to hold a hook; threading line through it will prevent line from releasing off the reel, no matter how beautifully cast; see page 34 for more on this!), and learning to fly fish is a lot less frustrating in the company of others.

My friend tied a short piece of knitting yarn to my line (my twig idea wasn't so smart after all) and stood day after day in a parking lot with me as I learned to give my rod a quick snap up to the back, pause, then finish with a firm, but not rushed, forward release. I spent hours practicing miles away from water. For a while I contemplated never actually fishing: the casting itself was a glorious motion, the line whispering as it shot past my ear, tracing graceful arcs in the sky.

But to the water I went. The first time I felt a tug on my line my heart jumped and stayed thumping for seconds. Was it fear or joy? The pulls and yanks on the line connected me to a life, vital and mysterious, surging to and fro. The fly line was our connection, and as I slowly reeled in that line the still morning of the pond vanished, leaving me dreading the inevitable encounter. And yet when the glistening, fluttering little sunfish broke the surface, I knew why I fished. I am there to meet fish, to hold them in my mind's eye as they swim away, back to the cool depths.

Learning to fly fish introduced me to a new world. Now I'll watch an insect hatch on my pond, mesmerized by the small rings of water signifying the rise of a fish to feed. I'll haul up a pile of muck from the pond bottom and search for insect pupae. But mostly I study the water, day in and day out, at dawn and again at twilight, hoping to grasp the habits of fish, to learn what they eat and when. And then I try to make my fly emulate those insects, working to land it quietly and elegantly on the pond's surface.

Why a book on fly-fishing for women? Because if you're like me, you welcome a different approach, one that includes the voices of others who are also learning a new sport. Gear, clothing, and certain issues—like safety precautions when fishing alone—are just different for us. Not to mention that it's fun to learn with like-minded folk. So let Dana introduce you to the world of the female fly fisher. In this book she'll teach you how to thread your fly line the right way, cast to perfection, and how to find the perfect pair of waders for the female form.

What's so different about the way women learn? If you're like me, you want to hear a description of a method or tactic before launching into it. I'm a fan of the talk-it-over-and-think-it-through-first school of learning. I prefer to ask questions before I'm asked to stand waist deep in a rushing stream waving a stick around. I want to hear advice from someone who thinks like I do. And I like to learn in a group so I can hear other folks' questions—and know I'm not the only one wondering how to tell a Woolly Bugger from a Royal Wulff (see pages 36–38).

We've done our best to mimic the learning conditions of a woman's instructional clinic in The Ragged Mountain Press Woman's Guides. There's a sense of camaraderie, honesty, and just plain fun. Here you'll find lots of women's voices: your instructor's, of course, but also voices of women from all walks who love the outdoors. *Fly Fishing: A Woman's Guide* provides solutions, advice, and stories from women who have done what you are about to do: learn to fly fish. I hope Dana's words and approach help get you out exploring and enjoying, by yourself or with a friend. I'll look for you out there.

Between fly-fishing trips, drop us a note to tell us how we're doing and how we can improve these guides to best suit you and your learning style.

MOLLY MULHERN GROSS
Series Editor, The Ragged Mountain Press Woman's Guides
Camden, Maine
May 1999

An avid outdoorswoman, Molly Mulhern Gross enjoys running,
hiking, camping, sea kayaking, telemark skiing, in-line skating,
biking, and snowboarding. She is Director of Editing, Design,
and Production at Ragged Mountain Press and International Marine.

CONTENTS

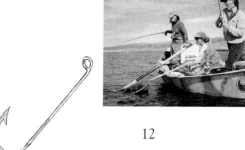

Acknowledgments 12

Introduction 13

Chapter 1: Women and Fly-Fishing 15

What is fly-fishing? 15

Why fly-fishing? 16

Who fly fishes? 18

Chapter 2: Getting Started 22

What does it take? 22

Physical profile 24

Solo or with others? 24

Classes and schools 25

Classes for women 26

Acquiring gear 27

Common concerns 28

Chapter 3: Your First Excursion 30

Getting comfortable on the water 30

Rods and gear 31

Other basic items 35

Where to go 40

What else do I need to know? 43

Chapter 4: Basic Techniques 45

Why is casting so important? 45

Casting theory 46

What you need for casting practice 47

The basic cast 48

Troubleshooting 54

More advanced casting concepts 57

Chapter 5: Advanced Techniques 63

From the fly line to the fly 63

Knots 68

 CONTENTS

Fly-fishing strategy 71
The catch 85
Protecting our resources 87

Chapter 6: Equipment 91
Selecting a fly rod 91
Selecting a reel 96
Fly lines 99
Dress for success 102
Waders 105
Vests 110
Alternatives to a vest 115
Landing nets 115
Putting it all together 117

Chapter 7: Personal Safety and Outdoor Skills 119
Wading 119
Feeling safe as a woman 122
Stream etiquette 125
Personal comfort 126

Chapter 8: Further Adventures 128
Expanding your adventures 128
Pregnancy and other special physical conditions 133
Fly-fishing with children 135

Chapter 9: Real Bugs, Flies You Tie, and Final Thoughts 137
Aquatic entomology 137
Fly selection 142
Fly-tying basics 144
Final thoughts 145

Chapter 10: Resources 147

Index 151

Acknowledgments

When my call for help went out to the many women fly fishers that I've met through teaching and guiding fly-fishing, women from all over the country took time to share their thoughts and feelings about the sport that binds us together. Barriers that often divide us—married or single, with or without children, young or old—were all stripped away; I felt a bond with each woman because we are fly fishers. Thank you all for sharing your thoughts and stories with me. Your love of fly-fishing and the enthusiasm you shared were often the inspiration I needed to keep working on this project.

I have many people to thank for giving me encouragement and convincing me that I had to write this book. I've decided that writing is like running a marathon. After the initial thrill you begin to wonder why you started in the first place, and then as you come down the homestretch, it becomes crystal clear. I thank Jeff Serena, who was responsible for getting me started on this journey and whose quiet patience and persistence guided me toward my goal. I also thank Molly Mulhern Gross, whose vision created this series, and all the folks at Ragged Mountain Press who helped me make a book from a rough, rough draft. Special thanks go to Jim and Martha Cannon, whose support and understanding helped me to hang in there. I am grateful to Mark Harrington for all his encouraging words and for allowing me the time I needed away from my other full-time job to complete this work, and to all of my friends from the Blue Quill Angler, whose friendship and fishing stories have helped to fill these pages.

Special thanks to Jean Williams for her superb modeling skills in so many of the book's photographs, and to Chris Hill for modeling the float tube shots. To Gil Alfring: thank you for your photographic talents—and to B. J. Lester: I so appreciate your help for providing the photographs of the flies. Thanks also to Mike Clough and all the folks at Orvis for their support.

Thank you, Dad, for getting me started in this crazy sport and for teaching me how to be patient, through your patience with me. And thank you, Mom, for teaching me that life and everything in it is not a product but a process, to be cherished along the way.

I knew I was in trouble when I began to dream about fly-fishing. Unable to fall asleep at night, I'd close my eyes and picture the river, see the sun reflecting off the water, hear the soothing and powerful roar of water making its way through moss-covered rocks. In my dream I'd put on my waders and gear, string up my fly rod, and ease my way into the water to make my first cast. Fly-fishing had become a passion, not just a pastime. I was hooked.

Fishing has always been a part of my life. My grandparents were anglers. For vacations, they packed their camper and traveled to every lake in northern California to fish. When I was three, I permanently borrowed my older brother's Zebco spin rod and spent hours in the backyard, zinging out that black and white bobber as far as I could, attempting to hit the neighbor's fence. My father was thrilled that I showed an interest in fishing, and he decided that we would become fly fishers.

When I was starting out, there weren't any classes available that I knew of, so I muddled my way through, teaching myself. I hated it at first! I couldn't get the fly to go where I wanted it to, and I caught more bushes than trout. But the challenge to become proficient remained. As I continued my attempts to better my skills, with my dad's encouragement and annoying persistence, I began to wean myself off my spin-fishing gear. I wanted to look like those fly fishers I saw standing in the water, the silver line traveling through the air with ease and elegance. When I made a conscious decision to leave my spin gear behind, I was on my way to the lifetime learning and appreciation of the skills and strategy involved in fly-fishing.

As I was refining my skills, I became a fly-fishing fanatic, fishing at every opportunity. I spent every vacation traveling to the mountains in search of trout-filled streams. I was working at a job fifty weeks of the year to be able to do what I really wanted to be doing—fly-fishing—for the other two weeks. Then, after a particularly stressful day on the job, it hit me like a bolt of lightning: I wanted work I was passionate about. I wanted to work outdoors with people. Standing at that crossroads in my life, I decided that I wanted to teach and guide fly-fishing for a living.

The reviews were mixed: "You want to do what?!" My family and close friends thought it was a crazy yet wonderful idea; others thought it would never work out. I tried not to let the skeptics hold me back. I was determined to become a professional fly fisher. I have no regrets about my choice, but it has not always been an easy road. There were not many women role models to look to, and I wondered why. Were women afraid to go fly-fishing alone or of being the only woman out there? Did women need different equipment? Were there things I needed to know because I was a woman?

When I started teaching and guiding, I enjoyed feeling unique as a woman pursuing a career in fly-fishing, yet I wanted to be more than a novelty. I wanted to be recognized for my skills and passion for the sport, not just because I was a woman. It was a struggle. At first I tried to be just "one of the boys," but that didn't work well because I was clearly different. Although the men I met openly welcomed me into their circles, some quite frankly didn't know what to do with me. I yearned to find and share experiences with other women who were making a living in this business traditionally dominated by men.

As time went on, I discovered that there *are* in fact many women who fly fish and who are role models in the sport, guiding, teaching, and working in fly-fishing shops. Yet although their numbers increase every year, I often wonder why there aren't even more. In searching for the answer to that question, I have asked other women anglers, "Why do we enjoy fly-fishing?" and hoped their reasons would help persuade others to try it. Women have been fishing throughout history. Who knows where along the way fly-fishing turned into a male-oriented sport?

Today, though, women have more freedom to do what we want than ever before, and fly-fishing is something many of us want. In October 1998, in Sun Valley, Idaho, I attended the Third Annual International Festival of Women Fly Fishers with more than 100 women from all over the country, and their interest and enthusiasm were overwhelming. I observed that what set the festival apart from all-male or coed fly-fishing groups was that these women were there to celebrate their uniqueness and their camaraderie as well as their love of the sport. It wasn't about conquest or sharing fish pictures, boasting the biggest or the most; it was about the simple joy of recognizing that we were of all different backgrounds, ages, and abilities and yet were bonded together by our common passion: from west to east, north to south, we were women who loved to fly fish. I invite you to join us. Welcome to the world of fly-fishing!

Chapter 1

WOMEN AND FLY-FISHING

WHAT IS FLY-FISHING?

I have often heard people say that fishing is boring: you cast the line out, and then while you're waiting for the fish to bite, you read a book or work on your tan. Or they say fishing is dirty: they don't like to get that "stuff"—worms, salmon eggs, or other slimy bait—on their hands. Well, I don't either! But that's where fly-fishing is different.

> **Y**ou don't just observe the outdoor world; you are in it. Fly-fishing involves all the senses—the feels, sights, smells, sounds.

Fly-fishing is a method of enticing fish with imitations of their natural food, such as insects and small fish. *Flies* are hand-tied from feathers, fur, fabric, or whatever will make them look to a fish like the real edibles it sees on or under the water. These materials are fastened to a hook with wraps of thread.

Many tied flies, such as a pattern representing a mosquito, are virtually weightless and therefore require some means of *presentation*, or getting them to the fish. This is done by casting a weighted line through the air so the fly will land naturally on the water. In a good presentation the imitation fly not only looks but acts like the real insect. It sounds simple in theory but involves a lot of skills, from figuring out what fly to use and developing an accurate cast to finding out where the fish are feeding. It's also helpful if you practice being patient and persistent.

WHY FLY-FISHING?

Fly-fishing is just plain fun and—unlike bait fishing—always gives you something to do. If you sometimes take a break to suntan and relax, it won't be because you are bored from a lack of activity. The enjoyment comes at many levels, and it's different for everyone. From a purely results-oriented perspective, catching fish is always enjoyable, but fly-fishing is an entire process, and all of it is interesting.

It starts with being a good observer. What kinds of insects do you see flying in the air above the water? Are there birds swooping down to take insects off the surface? You learn how to read the water, or to understand that fish will favor different types of water at different times. On the basis of all this you learn to try different flies until you find one that works better than another. And then sometimes you'll find that after all your observation and study about what should and should not be working, you must just trust your intuition or follow a hunch.

Fly-fishing is also about the enjoyment of just being out there, on or in the water. As a friend once said to me, trout live in beautiful places. When you fly fish, you become a part of those places. You don't just observe the outdoor world; you are in it. Fly-fishing involves all the senses—the feels, sights, smells, sounds. You get to slosh around in the water, which sometimes means getting your boots stuck in the mud. You'll be gazing in the water looking for signs of fish and notice a sparkling rock embedded with fool's gold. You'll watch leaves fall to the water on crisp golden autumn days and savor the smell of sweet wood smoke in the air. You might find yourself out in the middle of wet snowstorms in April, when the world is muffled and insulated, and the snow sticks to your hat and glasses.

One brisk morning when the sun hit the river and the steam was rising like smoke, I heard a great splash and looked up to see a deer leap through the water and jump up on the opposite bank. And here on this side was a fawn, looking panicked until she saw her mother on the other side of the river. Then she too bounded across to safety.

Every outing is a new adventure. A typically quiet and stealthy friend of mine once burst

- -

"Fly-fishing is an art to discover and constantly master. But it is also a song of the senses and a celebration of the spirit. For me, the actual landing of the fish is secondary to the total experience. My only regret is that I waited so long to discover this sport."

—Glenda Smith, age 51

- -

excitedly through the brush where I was fishing: "You'll never believe what I saw!" He went on to tell me that as he was approaching a pool, he heard great splashing, too large a disturbance for a fish to make, so he dropped to his hands and knees and crawled toward the sounds. He saw a wake in the water, and suddenly out popped a little brown, wet head with tiny black eyes that stared back at him with curiosity. The head vanished, and then two heads appeared. As my friend watched, a whole family of river otters, five in all, crawled up on a rock to see who had come to visit their home.

Fly-fishing is a "time-out" from the hustle and bustle of day-to-day living. When I'm fishing, I have time to let my mind wander and move at my own pace. All my worries are put on hold while I'm thinking about that next cast and anticipating the new and exciting water and sights just around the next bend.

Fly-fishing can also be a mental game. I have often described it as problem solving; the challenge is to determine if there are fish, where they are, what they are feeding on, and how best to entice them with what fly. "When it all comes together," says Gracia Barry, 53, "I feel a great sense of accomplishment and pride."

It's wonderful as well to know you can share both your triumphs and frustrations. Fly-

Fly-fishing with friends can be a joy.

"**W**ith the daily routine, we are faced with this and that fear or frustration. Getting out on the river enables me to focus on the beauty and rhythm of nature; the spirit of the river seems to heal and make me feel whole again."

—Cathy Tronquet, age 49

fishing can be a great way to spend time with friends, while you fish or when the day is done. There's something about sitting around a campfire or around the table at night, drinking coffee and telling stories of the day, some hilarious, some touching. Even the most hardened angler has some memory to share, and your own enjoyment is heightened by the pure excitement in your friend's eyes as he or she relives a moment.

There are times when your focus is just on the fishing. Gail Corkern, 50, sums it up: "Simply put, I fish to catch fish. This is both a pleasure and a source of frustration where fly-fishing is concerned. During a recent fishing trip, a group of friends were sitting around after dinner, discussing why it was that they fly fished. They suggested many reasons, the outdoors, the serenity, the scenery, the escape from the responsibilities of everyday life. After having considered all of their

> **F**ish on! There is nothing else like the rush of adrenaline that comes in knowing you are connected to a fish by a very thin line.

reasons, I still came to the conclusion that I fish to catch fish (and release them to be caught another day)."

There are days however, when you have tried everything in your fly box by every possible method, and still—no fish. Those are the days when I just scratch my head. But this puzzlement is also part of the mystique and joy of fly-fishing. It gives me plenty to think about on the car ride home and inspires me to plan for next time. There are a lot of "next times" in fishing—fly-fishing is hopeful that way. You know you will go back, armed with a new arsenal of flies or a new technique to try.

WHO FLY FISHES?

In *Reel Women: The World of Women Who Fish*, Lyla Foggia embraces the colorful, significant contributions women have made to the history of fishing. She includes both historical vignettes of women who were pioneers in fly-fishing and stories of contemporary women who are still breaking down barriers or preconceived notions of what women can accomplish in the sport. All these independent women, regardless of what was thought of as acceptable or considered the norm, went on to pursue their goals and dreams in the world of fishing.

As I began meeting women fly fishers, I was surprised by their varied backgrounds. Clearly, there was not a "type" of woman who fly fished. There was a range of ages, experiences, and vocations. But all the women shared a common bond: the love of being outdoors.

Some said it was the soothing sound of rushing water, others said it was the quiet they enjoyed the most. "I have loved nature, wildlife, forests, streams, mountains, beaches all of my life," Laurie Halsey, age 57, explains. "My husband and I have created our lifestyle—home, family, vocations and avocations—around the out-of-doors, and we and our children truly grew up fly-fishing."

One 78-year-old woman brought her 14-year-old grandson to a parent-and-child fly-fishing class so she could have a fishing buddy. She and her husband shared a passion for the outdoors, and after he passed away, she decided she was too young to give up the fly-fishing she had loved all her life. Once her grandson learned how, she didn't have to give it up, and they could spend time together.

Kathy Young, 46, emphasizes "letting your hair down and living for the simplest of needs. I find fly-

Fly-fishing can be a way to get back in touch with nature.

fishing so earthy and real. You don't worry about your makeup, clothes, or hair. You keep your identity as a woman but without adornment."

Many of my students start out thinking that they have come just to learn how to fly fish, but during the course of the day a most amazing transformation happens. I see the lines of trouble and worry on their faces begin to fade away, replaced by an enthusiasm and excitement that was not there before. When they hook into their first trout, their eyes are as bright as a child's on Christmas morning.

Wonderful things happen to people on the river. Several couples came to one fly-fishing class to learn together. At first, the ringleader, a domineering older man, was very vocal and demanding about what he expected in return for his money. He was barking out orders for both me and his friends, and I thought to myself, "Oh boy, this is going to be a really long day." As the lesson went on, however, his tensions seemed to be washed away by the soothing sights and sounds of the river. He actually began to laugh and enjoy himself; he became a completely different person. As the day was coming to a close, his wife explained to me that her husband had been going through some difficult times with his career and family. With tears in her eyes, voice trembling, she said that this was the happiest and most relaxed she had seen him in years.

One of my favorite stories is of two best friends who "abandoned" their husbands and children for a fly-fishing trip of their own. They had once been neighbors but over time had moved to different parts of the country, so this was a reunion of sorts. One had been fly-fishing for several years with her husband and wanted to introduce her best friend to the sport. I will always remember the two of them hugging and crying tears of joy in the middle of the river over catching a beautiful, wild brown trout together. "There is nothing like sharing fly-fishing with a good friend," one of them told me later. "We get so excited talking about Woolly Buggers, a new way to tie a knot, or how fly-fishing nourishes our souls. Our friendship and our fishing adventures can only be described as gifts in my life." Those two women now plan an annual fly-fishing excursion, traveling to different destinations in order to spend time together.

Jill Anthony, 46, says she "took up fly-fishing in self-defense! When my husband and I hiked to mountain lakes, he would carry his rod and flies, and I became his 'spotter.' That was fun for the first hour. But one hour would stretch into two or three, and I finally decided that if you can't lick 'em, you might as well join 'em."

A retired woman from Wisconsin who had moved to Florida decided she wanted to travel

> "**F**ly-fishing forces me to be patient, quiet, and focused. I have found great peace in quietly looking for fish, patiently tying on flies, and focusing on the water. One cannot be in a hurry! When I'm feeling as fragmented as an unassembled jigsaw puzzle, a day of fishing helps to integrate me and instill a sense of wholeness."
>
> —Kathy Young, age 46

EVEN FISHLESS DAYS ARE ADVENTURES

One day my brother and I packed up his truck and set out on a four-hour drive that ended up taking us more than five hours to reach a destination we had read about. But getting there was half the adventure. We took wrong turns and had to back track after we tried to go around one side of a reservoir that led us only to a dead end. All the while I was thinking, "Are we ever going to get there? Where is there?"

We finally arrived at a beautiful section of river, and as I stepped out of the truck I could smell the freshness of the oak leaves and hear the roar of the water. We were surrounded by rolling foothills framed by the dark purple, rugged granite of the Sierra Nevada. We rigged our rods and proceeded to fish.

We didn't hook or even see a fish that day, but my brother and I spent hours trying to catch a crayfish that kept chasing our flies. Drift after drift, that little crayfish would come out of its hiding place and move our flies away from where we had worked so hard to set them down. Finally we decided to try to hook the crayfish, instead!

(continued next page)

Women who fly fish enjoy the sport at many different levels: being outdoors in the fresh air, sharing another's company, having a time to reflect, or simply catching a fish. Everyone's experience will be unique. Go out there and make it the experience you want.

around the country, see old friends, and do some things she had never had a chance to try. She put all her belongings in storage, bought a minivan (equipped with a cellular phone at her daughter's urging), and came to our fly-fishing school. I admired this woman because even in her 70s she had a nothing-can-stop-me attitude.

I met another woman, bubbling with enthusiasm about fly-fishing, who said when she turned 50 she had thought sadly, "now I'm too old to learn." The minute she said it, she realized how silly that was, because if she got started right away, she'd have at least 30 years of good fishing ahead of her! She has been at it for several years now and looks forward to a lifetime of fly-fishing experiences.

Many women get started in fly-fishing in order to do something for themselves after giving so much time and nurturance to husbands, family, and children. Nancy Wickes, age 72, told me she had always wanted to fly fish, and one snowy winter day, depressed by the recent death of her husband, she forced herself to make arrangements to learn. "I called the local tackle shop: 'I know it's a Saturday morning and there's snow on the ground, but do you have a guide available to teach an old lady how to fly fish?' In twenty minutes I was in the car and on my way to the shop. I was immediately put at ease by my appointed guide, who helped me into the proper gear. I must say I didn't look very attractive in oversized waders, too large boots and jacket, and funky hat, but off we went. I am a skier and a tennis player, but fly-fishing has taken precedence in my life."

Once you learn how, fly-fishing can be a lifetime sport. Even if you take time off from it, you can come back to it years

Fly-fishing guide Kim Keeley finds serenity on a river.

later and it will still be there. A friend who went fly-fishing on a pond just two weeks before giving birth to her son has not had a lot of time for it since then, but when she finds time again, she can choose to pick up where she left off.

Women who fly fish enjoy the sport at many different levels: being outdoors in the fresh air, sharing another's company, having time to reflect, or simply catching a fish. Everyone's experience will be unique. Go out there and make it the experience you want.

EVEN FISHLESS DAYS ARE ADVENTURES

• • • • • • • • • • • • • • • • • •

(continued from previous page)

But we weren't successful in that endeavor, either. We took turns carefully presenting a fly in just the right place. The water was crystal clear and shallow, so we could watch the entire drama unfold. The crayfish would try to grab the fly in its claw and several times actually appear to be hooked. We would pull it in and even manage to lift it completely out of the water, only to have it fall back in with a "splat."

The main thing I remember about that day was laughing so hard my stomach hurt. That and spending time playing with my brother as we did when we were kids. I have had other outstanding fishing days when I hooked and landed several trophy-sized fish. But I will always remember the whimsical adventure of that fishless day as one of my favorites.

Chapter 2

GETTING STARTED

> "In fly-fishing, success is dependent not on brawn and size but on technique and finesse."
>
> —Beth Parento, age 25

WHAT DOES IT TAKE?

Fly-fishing is a sport in which women can excel because there are so few physical barriers. Regardless of age, body type, or muscular condition, virtually anyone who wants to can learn to fly fish. In fact, many say that women make better fly fishers than men because so many aspects of the sport, particularly casting and playing fish, have to do with skill and experience rather than sheer power.

Fly-fishing involves not only learning the actual skills to fish but also being comfortable outdoors. Many women who enjoy hiking or camping naturally extend their outdoor interest to fly-fishing. True, the weather doesn't always cooperate; days may be dry and blistering hot, windy and cold, raining or snowing. A friend of mine proclaims that she is only a fair-weather fisher and won't even consider a fishing trip unless it's spring or summer or a golden day in late fall. You certainly don't have to fly fish in weather or conditions that make you miserable; that choice is part of being able to make your own rules. But even in fair weather there can be less-than-pleasant elements to contend with, such as biting ants or mosquitoes. You need to realize that fly-fishing puts you right out there with *all* of nature's creatures.

• •

You don't have to spend countless hours on and off the water before you can be successful.

• •

I want to learn!

The next thing it takes is the willingness to learn. I have met women who had been so pressured to love fly-fishing that they became stubbornly resistant to learning how. If they did go along, they always relied on a husband, boyfriend, or male family member to tie their knots, choose the water, make all the plans. In talking with these women, I found that they had all perceived someone else as the expert. The women themselves had not learned much about what they were doing; they just did what they were told! But you don't have to rely on someone else. Nor do you have to conduct years of research and study to be successful. The willingness to acquire some basic skills and knowledge will give you the tools to be independent and become more proficient at fly-fishing.

Confidence through knowledge

I'm an advocate of gaining confidence through knowledge in any pursuit but especially in learning a new skill. Other women fly-fishers tell me the reason there are not more women out there on their own is that many are intimidated. They are fearful of being surrounded by others, mainly men, who appear to know what they are doing. They are afraid—as Glenda Smith, 51, admitted—of "looking inept and inexperienced. But as I've learned more and felt my confidence grow, I'm not bothered by that anymore."

Don't worry! Learn the basics, and with knowledge, you will gain confidence and have a better idea of what you are trying to do. You don't have to spend countless hours on and off the water before you can be successful. The information that you gather and the skills you acquire tend to stay with you, even if you're able to get out only a few times a year—though of course the more you go out and the more you use your skills, the easier it all becomes, especially such things as tying knots and casting.

BLACK CLOUDS

• • • • • • • • • • • • • • • •

On a fishing and camping adventure with my family in northern California, in the year of a major drought, we traveled to a lake we had fished many times before, only to find the water a few hundred feet away from the dried, cracked shoreline and beached boat ramps. We stopped in the parking lot, and my dad and brother got out of the car to scout the water for fishing. As they ran toward the water, I remember seeing a black cloud form around each one like an aura. As they got farther away from the car, I watched as their arms were flailing around their heads, in the air. I looked out and saw the same black cloud forming around the car. We were under attack! Thousands of mosquitoes in a tornado-like swarm were trying to draw blood out of my dad, my brother, and the warm car engine. As much as I love fly-fishing, I wasn't about to get out of that car! There are times that you have to decide just how much you will endure from the natural elements in order to fish.

PHYSICAL PROFILE

Physically, I enjoy the agility required to scramble among rocks along the river and the balance it takes to walk across the water on logs. I much prefer to get my workout for the day by climbing up and down hills to reach the water than by spending time on a health club stair-stepping machine. And I have a friend who won't fly fish anywhere near a paved road; she'll hike miles into the backcountry to enjoy her fly-fishing experience. If you choose, then, fly-fishing can be physically demanding, but it doesn't have to be. One of the great things about the sport is that you don't have to be in top-notch cardiovascular shape. I see fly fishers who are from all parts of the country, rural and urban. They come from different climates and are in differing degrees of physical shape. For some, being at altitude in the mountains may cause discomfort.

Fly-fishing in remote or hard-to-get-to high mountain lakes or streams can be a beautiful experience, but it's not for everyone. (For the symptoms of altitude sickness, see chapter 7.) Pick and choose your terrain based on what you like and what you can do.

There are many places where access to the water is not difficult, even if you have, say, a bad knee or hip. Find a river or lake where the access is a gradual slope or primarily flat.

One woman's eyes were bright and excited as she told me stories of fly-fishing trips with her husband and children. When I asked where she had fished recently, she explained that a bad knee had prevented her from getting out for several years. Sadly, she seemed resigned to the prospect that she could never fly fish again. It was obvious to me that she missed it, so we talked about places where she could have easy access to a river or lake. I suggested that perhaps she could fly fish from a boat or a float tube, an inflated device designed for anglers (see chapter 8).

There are a lot of great fishing spots alongside roads. I choose these places when I have limited time or just don't feel like making the extra effort to hike. The sounds of the water serve to muffle any vehicle noise.

SOLO OR WITH OTHERS?

Fly-fishing is one sport that doesn't require getting a team or a crew together in order to do it. It's fun to have friends to fish with, but unlike volleyball or tennis, you can have fun with it on your own. When you do go out with others, you can fish side by side all day, but more likely you'll find that you fish together some of the time and apart some of the time, even if you can still see your fishing partner. It's nice to have the companionship of another and also have the freedom to fish your own water.

It does help to have a partner when you're getting started, someone to help motivate you to go out. Two women I know have a standing weekly fishing date; no matter the weather or schedule demands, they set aside their day of the week to go fly-fishing. We're all different in how we want to pursue a new interest. Some of you may want to learn as much as you can on your own and start by reading, renting videos, or just getting out there to fish. Others may prefer to join a group that has planned activities so you can share fly-fishing with friends. (For reading sources and fly-fishing groups, see chapter 10.)

CLASSES AND SCHOOLS

The best thing you can do when you are getting started is to take a class or attend a beginning fly-fishing school. There are such schools all over the country, and many courses are taught through community colleges and in local fly shops.

It's important that you get started with quality instruction. Before you sign up for a class, here are some questions that you should ask:

- **Who teaches the class?** What experience do the instructors have? How long have they been teaching? You want to learn from someone who has had both teaching and fishing experience. The best fly fishers don't always make the best instructors.

- **What kind of fly-fishing is emphasized?** There are classes that specialize in saltwater fly-fishing, which will not be appropriate if what you want is to fish trout streams.

- **What is the class size?** If there are more than 8 or 10 students for each instructor, you might want to find a smaller class to get more individualized instruction.

- **What is the format?** Will we actually go out to fly fish on water? Many skills can be taught on dry land or in the classroom, but find a program that includes trips to both a stream and a pond or lake, so you experience both moving and still water.

- **What will I learn about?** The classroom curriculum should include casting, equipment (rods and reels and essential gadgets), knots and line setup, and basic aquatic entomology (the life

---

IT PAYS TO START RIGHT

• • • • • • • • • • • • • • • • • • • •

When my husband bought his first fly rod, he didn't catch as much as my own previous fishing experience had led me to expect. How could one spend so much time up to his hips in water and catch so little? After I caught my first fish on a fly rod, the guide standing right at my elbow, I was convinced that I could do it again any time I wanted to. We returned a week later with the same flies to the same river and didn't catch a single fish! What was most frustrating was that I could see beautiful fish swimming around my feet, yet no matter what I did, I couldn't get a single one to take a fly. I was outraged! I decided that I would not be outsmarted by a fish whose brains are the size of a pea—a small pea at that. I began to read and to attend fly-fishing classes offered by our local fly shop. I was amazed at the amount there was to learn and at the subtleties of this sport, especially compared with other kinds of fishing. I do better now.

—Gail Corkern, age 50

cycles of water insects). On field trips you should be taught stream and wading safety, how to fish by different methods, and how to play and release fish properly.

- **What do I need to bring?** Some schools provide a fly rod and waders for class use; others do not. Find out what equipment and supplies are included and where you can rent equipment if need be.

- **How much can I expect to pay?** Community college or recreation center classes are the most affordable way to go, with a fee of about $50. Although classes taught by fly-fishing professionals may cost more, at $100 to $395, they should have a smaller student-to-instructor ratio, and you are likely to get better instruction. Ask what additional costs to expect for items such as flies and tackle, or fees for a river outing or going to private water.

You might decide it's worth the extra money to travel to a school that is recognized throughout the country for its expert instruction. A class such as those offered by the Orvis Fly-Fishing Schools (see chapter 10) is a great way to get started. The Orvis schools teach fly-fishing for all species, from cold-water (trout and salmon) to warm-water (bass, bluegill) to saltwater fish. The classes are taught at various sites throughout the country, including Vermont, Colorado, Massachusetts, New York, and Florida. No matter how many books you read or people you talk to, nothing can take the place of a fishing experience with a qualified instructor by your side.

CLASSES FOR WOMEN

Many schools offer classes for women only (see chapter 10). Some of you may have had less than favorable experiences learning to fly fish with men, or you just may feel more comfortable learning in the company of other women. There are usually women in the coed groups, so it's likely that you'll have some female company. But I have taught both coed and women-only classes and teaching the women's classes is a highlight of my summer because the energy level is different. A cohesiveness and camaraderie develops right away. Women are truly able to speak their minds and ask questions without feeling the stigma of being "just a girl who doesn't get it"; in a women's class, everyone can be just a student who doesn't get it.

What's more, they help one another. One day when I took a women's class to a pond to practice casting and still-water strategies, the fishing was a bit slow for everybody but one woman. She had successfully landed her first two fish, and when she hooked a third, a student who hadn't yet caught anything was standing nearby, watching. As I was moving to assist the woman with the fish, I saw her hand the rod, with a fish on, to her classmate. She proceeded to instruct her fellow student how to hold the rod and how to play the fish. As I approached them, I overheard the more successful student encouraging the other, "Isn't that a great feeling, having a fish pull on your line?" Both women were beaming, one playing her very first fish and the other happy to have shared something.

ACQUIRING GEAR

To get started, you're going to need a fly-fishing outfit (rod, reel, and line), and I recommend that you wear a set of waders. If you are not yet ready to invest heavily in the sport, consider renting equipment from a local fly shop. Rental rods are usually the basic, more affordable models (although some shops may also rent demo rods, which will be the higher-end and the most current models). Shops generally charge $10 to $20 a day for these outfits. Renting gear gives you the option of trying various equipment before you buy.

Most fly-fishing shops will also rent *waders*, a waterproof garment worn right over your clothing. Waders will either have boots attached or include a separate pair. When you go for your fitting, take the same clothing that you plan to wear while fishing, including a variety of socks from thicker ones to longer ones, in order to find the most comfortable fit for the boot. (For more about what to wear and about equipment specifically designed for women, see chapter 6.)

Borrowing equipment from a friend is another option, but beware of borrowing a rod that feels heavy or has a grip too large for your hand. You can comfortably cast a rod of any length all day long, but casting a rod with an oversized grip for even a few hours will fatigue your hand. Grips come in different sizes, and it's important to use equipment that

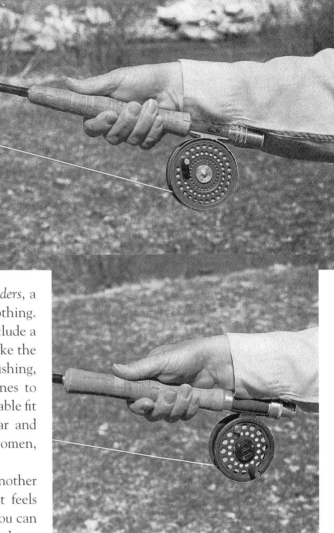

A **reversed half wells grip** on your rod (above) is smaller in diameter than the **full wells grip** (below) and is therefore a better choice for this angler's hand size.

fits you during your first time out so you won't become tired and frustrated. Starting out with the wrong gear has probably turned off more potential fly fishers than not catching any fish!

Finding used equipment is another possibility, but don't buy something just because it's cheap. Hand-me-down equipment is usually given away or on sale for a reason. Before purchasing any equipment, used or new, ask fly fishers you know what kind they have and what they would recommend. Ask questions at your local fly shop, too, and if there is none in your area, see chapter 10 for a list of manufacturers. The rod companies will of course be biased toward their own models, but you can ask them for general information about the length and weight of rod they recommend for the kind of fishing you plan to do. (See chapter 6 for details of equipment selection.)

Most fly-fishing shops will sell their end-of-season, used demo, or rental rods at a substantial discount, or you might find some great close-out bargains on discontinued models. The best time to look for these is in the fall or at the end of the busy summer season.

As with any purchase, the more time you invest in making your decision, the more likely you'll be satisfied with your choice down the road.

Although you may find a good deal on a rod, reel, and line starter package at a sporting goods or department store, a specialty fly-fishing store should have a more knowledgeable staff to educate you and help you with any questions. Simply put, fly-fishing stores specialize in fly-fishing, so seek out one with which to begin a relationship. Once a good fly shop's staff gets to know you as a customer and a friend, there is no better resource for good, current, honest information, not only about purchasing equipment but also about anything else related to fly-fishing.

COMMON CONCERNS

Here are some of the concerns common among people who are thinking about taking up fly-fishing. Many of your questions will be addressed in more detail in the chapters following.

- **Do I have to know how to swim?** Knowing how to swim will make you feel more confident around the water, but I know some fly-fishers who don't swim. You don't need to know how, but if you are planning to spend a lot of time fly-fishing, it would be a good idea to take at least a beginning swimming lesson that would include being comfortable floating and paddling around in the water.

- **What if I fall in the water?** Most falls will not be life threatening; the worst thing that will probably happen is that you get wet. Still, being safe is the first and most important thing to keep in the front of your mind when you are fly-fishing. The best way to avoid a dangerous fall is to avoid getting into a situation where you put yourself at risk. (See chapter 7 on wading safety.)

- **Will I hurt the fish?** Many fly fishers practice what is called catch-and-release fishing: instead of keeping a fish, they put it back into the water alive. If this is done properly, the fish won't be harmed. Catch-and-release fishing is a gratifying experience, knowing that the fish you released will live to reproduce and be there for you to catch another day. (See chapter 5 on releasing a fish.)

- **Will the fish hurt me?** Larger trout have teeth that can be sharp, but trout will not try to bite or attack you. Some other species such as pike or walleye, though, do have razor-sharp teeth and require special care. The actual handling of these fish is done with steel gloves, tools for spreading the mouth, and pliers to get the hook out.

- **Do I have to touch the fish?** Despite some people's belief, fish feel very firm, not mushy. All fish are coated with a thin layer of mucus that protects their bodies from infection and parasites. You will have to handle the fish, but minimal contact is advised, especially when releasing the fish live. Fish mucus washes off easily if you simply dip your hands in the water. A landing net is helpful to most anglers (see chapter 6).

- **What if I get a hook in me?** Spend enough time with sharp hooks, and eventually you will get one stuck in you. You must always wear glasses for eye protection when you fish, and a brimmed hat or baseball-style cap will also help to protect your face from stray lines and hooks. A hook embedded in your hand or other body part will hurt, but the effect will be greatly minimized if you have pressed down the barbule on all your flies and learned how to get a hook out if is lodged in you or your clothing (see page 86).

- **How will I ever learn to tell a dry fly from a nymph?** When you're first starting out, many flies may look similar. It is helpful to find a fly-fishing catalog with color pictures of different flies so that you can compare your flies with the ones pictured and labeled. The flies that you have may not look exactly like those in the catalog, but at least it will give you a general idea of what category your flies belong to.

- **Can I afford it?** Are there inexpensive ways to get gear and instruction for myself and my family? Although it is fun to take a beginning fly-fishing class together as a family, it may be more affordable for one adult to take a class and then share the knowledge with other family members. You might think about purchasing or renting only one rod, reel, and line and taking turns, letting one person use the rod while the others participate in such activities as birdwatching or hiking. Depending on the age and attention span of the children, they may need fill-in diversions, anyway.

- **Do I need a river to fly fish?** You can fly fish anywhere there is water that holds fish. If there are no rivers or creeks nearby, look for a pond or lake.

- **Do I need a boat?** A boat may provide you with better access to some areas of a lake, but it isn't necessary. In most locations you can fly fish from the bank or shore.

Chapter 3

YOUR FIRST EXCURSION

> "Just being outside in the fresh air with the stream roaring by, wading in the cold water with those awkward waders, is a pleasure. No competition, but just plain refreshing fun."
>
> —Bessie Armour, age 70

GETTING COMFORTABLE ON THE WATER

Fly-fishing, like many other sports, can be a continual learning process. As in any new activity, everything will probably feel awkward to you at first, from getting to know your equipment to wearing all the gear. But as Bessie Armour points out, "Just being outside in the fresh air with the stream roaring by, wading in the cold water with those awkward waders, is a pleasure. No competition, but just plain refreshing fun."

The amount of time it takes to become comfortable and then proficient in this sport will vary from one person to another. Much of this has to do with learning styles and with how often you are able to use what you learn. Are you a reader or a doer? I have found that most individuals tend to be both. Even information-gathering enthusiasts must at some point put some of that knowledge into practice.

If you are at all hesitant about going fly-fishing for the first time, all I can tell you is to go out there and enjoy your journey. From the planning phases of your trip all the way to the drive home, fly-fishing gives you an opportunity to get away and put life into perspective.

In the chapters to follow there's information you'll need to learn about casting, to help you put your fly where you want it; about "reading" the water, to help you identify places where fish are most likely to be; and about aquatic insects, to help you select the fly most likely to attract the fish you want to catch. But right now you just need some basic information for your first time out.

top guide

ferrule—male

snake guide

tip section

stripping guide

hook keeper

grip

reel seat

ferrule—female

butt section

butt cap

Parts of a fly rod.

RODS AND GEAR

For starters, you'll need a fly rod, a reel, and a fly line. The *fly rod* (remember to call it a rod, not a pole) is used to cast out a *fly line*, which is wound on a *reel*. Fly rods come in either two, three, or four pieces and in different lengths, weights, and flexes (see chapter 6).

Assembling the rod

Most rods will be enclosed in a tube or case, with or without the reel attached. If the reel is not attached, put the rod together first and then attach the reel (as explained below). If the reel is already attached, leave it there and read on about how to put the rod together.

In two-piece rods the smaller, top end is called the *tip section*, and the heavier section (the one with the handle, or *grip*) is called the *butt section*. All along both sections of the rods are metal eyes called *guides* through which the fly line is threaded. The connection between the pieces is called a *ferrule*, which consists of a male and a female part. To connect the rod, lightly set the tip end into the butt end. Instead of lining up the guides, set the tip section slightly askew from the butt. Place one hand on the tip section and the other on the butt section, about two inches from the ferrule, taking care not to use the guides as levers or handles. (The guides are attached to the rods with tight wraps of thread, covered with epoxy. Continued use of the guides as levers will eventually cause them to loosen and pop off the rod.) Twist and push the two parts together until the guides are in a line. The rod connection should be snug, not loose, but using too much force can cause the two rod parts to become difficult to separate. To undo the rod, reverse the process, gently twisting and pulling the rod apart.

To assemble a four-piece rod, use the same procedure but first put the top two sections together, set them aside while you put the bottom two sections together, then put the two resulting pieces together as if it were a two-piece rod.

For a three-piece rod, follow the same method, first putting the top two pieces together and

NO DISTRACTIONS

• • • • • • • • • • • • • • • • • • • •

Fly-fishing is a continual learning process, a constant challenge with great rewards. A day of fishing fills all my senses: the beauty and peace of the surroundings, the sound of the water rushing around rocks and past my legs, the cool water when wet-wading on a warm day, the challenge of casting and the concentration it takes to understand the river, the insects, and the habits of the fish, the surge of life on the end of the line when a fish decides to sample your offering. The water is the one place I can be in complete harmony with myself. I don't worry about outside events. Nowhere else am I so focused. Nowhere else do I experience that peace.

—Cathy Tronquet, age 49

When putting the rod together, set the tip section askew from the butt section and then twist the rod into alignment until it's snug but not too tight.

then attaching them to the butt section.

Attaching the reel

The place on the rod where the reel attaches is called the *reel seat*. There are different styles of reel seats. The bar across the reel is called a *foot*, which is designed to slide into an insert either under the grip or on a bracket away from the grip. The reel is secured by a ring on the opposite side to hold it in place. A *counterweight* allows the reel to rotate quickly without wobbling.

Before you proceed, you must decide which hand you'll reel with. Traditionally, a right-handed caster would cast with

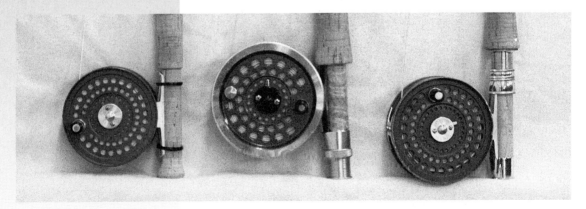

Left: The **cork and ring reel seat** actually has two rings. **Center:** The **uplocking reel seat** places the reel closer to the grip. **Right:** The **downlocking reel seat** locates the reel close to the end of the rod.

DISASSEMBLING A STUBBORN ROD

• •

If your rod is stuck together and cannot be pulled apart, there are two methods to separate the pieces without causing damage to the rod. Both methods involve keeping the rod straight as force is applied. Bending the rod while trying to get it apart may cause it to break.

By yourself (top right): Hold the rod horizontally behind your knees. This position provides the stability needed to prevent bending or torquing the rod. Slightly bend your knees and pull the rod apart in a straight line.

With a buddy (bottom right): If you cannot separate the rod by yourself, try this two-person method. Face your friend as if you were going to be in a tug-of-war. Have your partner place one hand on the tip section and one on the butt section, grasping the rod (not the guides) firmly. Position your hands next to hers, again using care not to grab the guides. Now, just as if you were pulling the rod apart by yourself, you both gradually apply force in a straight line in order to separate the pieces. Each of you stabilizes the other to prevent bending or torquing the rod. If you still cannot separate the parts, ask another person to join in so that three of you are pulling in unison.

line guard

counter-weight

spool release latch

handle

foot

Parts of a reel.

her right hand, pass the rod to her left hand, and then reel with her right hand. Unless you've already learned this sequence, however, I recommend that a right-handed caster learn to reel with the left hand; a left-handed caster, to reel with the right. This way, you are in better control of the rod, never having to change hands in order to reel in or retrieve line. If you are a right-handed caster, then, the reel should be attached so that the handle faces toward the left, and vice versa.

For more efficient and better controlled reeling, cast with your dominant hand but reel with your non-dominant hand: right-handed caster reeling with left hand (above) and left-handed caster reeling with right hand (left).

Most reels can be attached with the handle facing either right or left. Once you decide which way the reel should face, slide the reel foot into the slot and screw the locking ring so that it's snug. You do not need to overtighten. When the rod is assembled, hold it in your casting hand, allowing the reel to drop below your wrist.

Stringing up the rod

Once your rod is put together and the reel is attached, you're ready to string up the rod. Use care not to set the end of the rod that holds the reel in sand or fine dirt, as the grit will get inside the reel and cause it to rub or get stuck. (If this does happen, see chapter 6 on how to clean it out.) You can put the end of the rod on a bench, rock, grass, hat, or the car bumper in order to keep it free of grit.

Find the end of the line, pull a length of 10 or 12 feet from the reel, and let this line rest on the ground. Don't worry about getting it tangled.

Before you begin to thread the line, make sure that it is under the *line guard* on the reel and coming from the bottom of the reel. Then double the end of the line over to make a U shape and use it to thread through the guides, starting with the one that appears thicker than all the others. This is called a *stripping guide*. Note

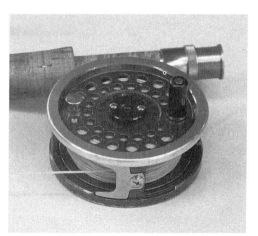

the location of the *hook keeper*. The hook keeper is not a guide through which you thread your line but serves as a latch to hook your fly to after the rod is threaded with fly line. Take your time while you are stringing up the fly rod, making sure that you have threaded every eye and that the line is not twisted around the rod. Check to make sure you've done this correctly before you tie your fly on; otherwise, you'll have to cut the fly off and rethread the rod.

Before threading the rod, make sure the fly line is coming off the outside bottom of the reel and under the **line guard**.

Thread the rod by pulling the fly line through the line guides with the line doubled over in a U shape. Latch your fly to the **hook keeper** (right) after threading the rod. Don't thread the fly line through the hook keeper.

OTHER BASIC ITEMS

Leaders

The line on the reel that you're working with may or may not have a leader attached; if not, you'll need to add one. A leader is a tapered length of monofilament or clear nylon line. The thick end of the leader attaches to the *butt section* (see page 31) of the fly line, which has a loop on the end.

Your fly is tied onto the thin end. The leader is clear so that it's virtually invisible to the fish.

Leaders come in different lengths and tapers. There are knotted leaders, but the knotless, tapered ones are more common. If you are fishing with very small flies, you will want a thin end. For, say, a grasshopper-sized fly you would need a thicker end. The thickness of the end of the leader is designated by a number followed by an X. The larger the number, say 6X, the finer the end. The smaller the number, the thicker the end. There is also a correlation between the thickness or X designation and the strength of the material (the smaller the number, the greater the strength). This *breaking strength*, measured in pounds of pressure, is the amount of pressure that can be applied before the material breaks. (For fuller explanation, see chapter 5.) For getting started, I recommend a tapered, knotless, 7½-foot-long, 4X leader.

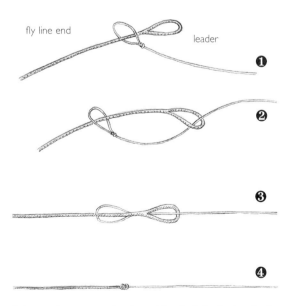

fly line end

leader

❶

❷

❸

❹

A **loop-to-loop connection** is used to attach the leader directly on the fly line. Insert the fly line loop through the leader loop (**1**). Insert the end of the leader through the fly line (**2**) and pull the connection tight (**3–4**).

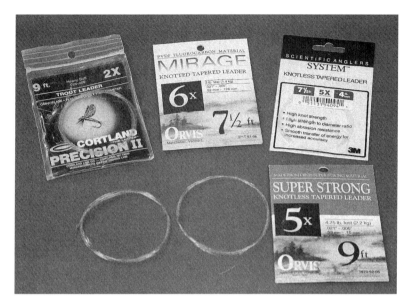

Different brands and types of leaders; make sure you use the length and taper suited to the type of fishing you plan to do.

Fly box

Fly-fishing uses not bait but lures called *flies*. Trout flies cost $1 to $3 per fly. The more expensive flies take more time to construct and are usually tied on better-quality hooks—sharper, stronger, and not so easily broken. There are many different types of flies in various sizes and colors (see chapter 9), but you need only a few to get started. Later you can learn which ones work best in what situations.

Flies that float on the surface of the water are called dry flies. Others that sink below the surface are called wet flies, nymphs, and streamers. All flies are meant to imitate a fish's natural food source.

Each type of fly has certain identifying characteristics. A traditional *dry fly* has feather fibers, called *hackle*, which radiate out from the straight part of the hook or shank at a 90-degree angle, looking like a lion's mane. The hackle imitates the wings and legs of a flying insect and enables the dry fly to float on the surface tension of the water. The *wet fly* may also have hackle and a wing, but the hackle is more sparse, and the wing and hackle appear swept or combed back from the eye of the hook. A *nymph* looks very compact and has a tapered silhouette, thinner at the end or bend of the hook and thicker toward the hook eye. Its construction may include gold or glass beads, and its body is sometimes wrapped with lead wire to make it sink. A *streamer* is made on a hook two or three times longer than the hooks used for other flies, and its longer lengths of material help it look like a small fish or leech.

All fly-fishing flies are referred to by size and a specific name. The size

. . . .

All flies are meant to imitate a fish's natural food source.

. . . .

Left to right: The four types of flies are dry fly, wet fly, nymph, and streamer.

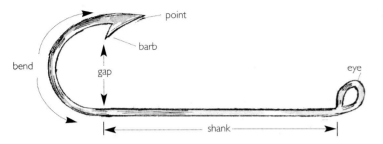

point

barb

bend

gap

eye

shank

Parts of a hook.

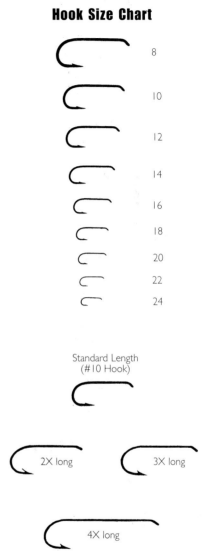

Hook Size Chart

8

10

12

14

16

18

20

22

24

Standard Length
(#10 Hook)

2X long

3X long

4X long

of the fly is determined by the size of the hook on which it is tied. The hooks range in size from #1/0 (pronounced "one aught"), used primarily for saltwater fly-fishing, all the way down to the very small #24, used mainly for fresh-water trout fishing. A fly's name may designate a certain river (Rio Grande Trude), or the person who tied it (Steve's Stonefly), or the insect it imitates (Black Gnat). There are also flies with descriptive names such as Irresistible or—from the materials used in its construc-tion—Gray Hackle Peacock. (For recommended flies in each category, see chapter 6.)

The easiest method for beginners is to fish with a dry fly on the fresh water of a pond, lake, or stream. (If you choose to start out in the salt water of the ocean or a bay, the use of a streamer is advised; see chapter 5.) With a dry fly you simply have to tie the fly on the end of your leader, and you can begin to fish.

To get started, I suggest that you purchase three to six dry flies, size #14. Recommended patterns include the Royal Wulff, Tan Elk Hair Caddis, Rio Grande Trude, and Royal Trude. All of these dry flies are easy to see on the

Left to right: You'll need a selection of flies such as Steve's Stonefly, Black Gnat, Irresistible, and Gray Hackle Peacock.

Left to right: The four recommended dry flies, Royal Wulff, Elk Hair Caddis, Rio Grande Trude, and Royal Trude are easy to see because they're light-colored and float well.

water because they are light in color and float well. Nymphs or streamers can also be tied right on the leader, but you will be more successful with these methods if you add weight. (For more details on fishing with different kinds of flies, see chapter 5.)

I also recommend that you purchase some fly flotant to apply to your dry flies before and during fishing. Flotant comes in a variety of forms including paste, gel, liquid, and dry crystals or powder (see page 113). Although dry flies are made to rest on the surface of the water, eventually they'll become saturated. Treating them with flotant will help them to float longer.

TYING THE FLY ON: CLINCH KNOT

To make a *clinch* knot, holding the fly in your nondominant hand, insert the end of the leader about 2 inches through the eye of the hook (**1**). Wrap the short end (tag end) around the long end (line end) five times (you can wrap either toward you or away from you, as long as you keep going in the same direction) (**2**). Take your tag end and insert it through the space in front of the hook eye (**3**). Pinch tag end between the thumb and forefinger where you are holding onto the fly. Moisten the wraps and pull on the line end only. Pull, don't bounce, this knot tight until you can feel the material stretch (**4**). Trim tag end with a snip (described under additional gadgets), leaving about 1/16 inch.

①

②

③

④

Additional gadgets

You'll need a few basic gadgets to get started. Some are optional items designed to make some task easier, such as knot-tying tools; others are essential for fishing. It's best to attach any small, often used tools to a retractor, sometimes called a zinger, which is a gadget with a retractable cord onto which you fasten smaller gadgets; otherwise, you will have a tendency to lose or misplace them.

You will need a *snip* to cut and trim your lines. A snip is a cutter that looks like a pair of fingernail clippers but is made of a stronger, rust-resistant metal and has a sharper blade that actually cuts the material, instead of crushing it. You'll find that line cut with a snip rather than a nail clipper is easier to thread through the eye of a fly's hook. Some fishing snips have an attached needle, which is useful to open an eye that gets blocked with glue or other material.

Another essential tool is a pair of *hemostats* or *forceps*. Forceps are used to press barbed hooks flat (see photo on page 86), to remove hooks from fish (and other places), and to help in tying knots. Selecting a pair with flat jaws, as opposed to

My polarized glasses are as important to my fishing as my fly rod and reel.

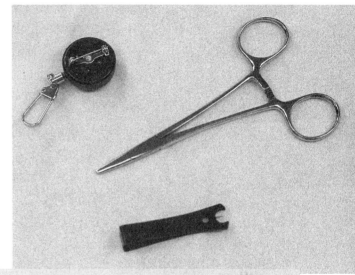

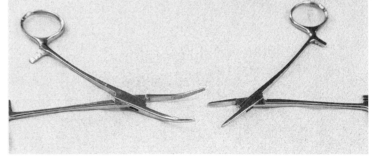

Top: Zinger, forceps, and snip are essential tools. **Above:** Forceps can have **serrated jaws** (left) or **flat jaws** (right).

serrated jaws, will enable you to work most effectively with all sizes of hooks. The serrated jaws have a tendency to damage smaller hooks.

I also urge you to wear a pair of polarized sunglasses to protect your eyes not only from the sun but from stray lines and hooks. Of course, any pair of sunglasses will serve, but polarized lenses are processed to eliminate glare from the water, allowing you to see underwater more effectively. This is essential for safe wading and for spotting fish. I was surprised to find that most expensive sunglasses are not polarized. To find out if yours are, take them to a fishing shop, which will probably have a display that you can view through your glasses to see whether or not they are polarized. My polarized glasses are as important to my fishing as my fly rod and reel.

GETTING STARTED CHECKLIST

For the purposes of getting started, I recommend the following equipment selections:

- 8- to 9-foot, 5- or 6-weight rod with reel and line
- 7½-foot, 4X leader (you might want to have an extra)
- 3 to 6 flies of size #14 (Royal Wulffs, Tan Elk Hair Caddis, Rio Grande Trudes, or Royal Trudes)
- flotant (optional, but recommended for dry flies)
- snips
- forceps
- polarized sunglasses

"The first time I caught a fish on my own, not only was I shocked when I felt the hit, but the feel and the sound of the line stripping off that reel was thrilling! I never knew one's heart could beat that fast! It is hard to describe the pure joy and rush when a fish is hooked and making a run for it. And the best part of the catch is still to come—the release. I don't have to feel guilty about harming or killing the fish, and I have preserved the gene pool."

—Jill Anthony, age 46

WHERE TO GO

Preparation is the key to your first time out. First, you should have a general plan where you're going and to what sort of water: large river, small creek, lake. I keep a file of places I've heard about, or have seen, that I'd like to try someday. Some require a lot of time to get to, but others aren't far. Don't feel you have to dedicate an entire day to your first time out. Depending on how much time you have for your fly-fishing adventure, start scheming.

The more often you can go out, the faster you will gain confidence. For your first few excursions it might be a good idea to go with someone who's fly fished before, but this is an activity you can do alone. In the beginning you might feel self-conscious, but just remember that the other anglers will likely be focused on their own fishing, not on watching you. You can watch them, however. A lot of my learning early on came through watching other anglers who made fly-fishing look graceful and easy. As Angie Jacobs, 32, told me, "I actually taught myself. I watched a lot of people fish successfully and unsuccessfully and just tried to incorporate the successful things into my fishing. I also asked and still ask my fishing friends a lot of questions and use their advice."

Types of water

When someone mentions fly-fishing, your mind is probably filled with images of high mountain lakes or fast-moving mountain trout streams. But fly-fishing is not just limited to that environment. Where do you live? The fly-fishing fundamentals can be used and applied in all climates and to many species of fish, although the specific gear, flies, and tactics may differ. This book does speak mainly to cold-water fishing, in water under 70°F, but warm water—defined by a temperature of 70° and above—is home to a whole world of other fish, including bass, bluegill, and crappie. You can fly fish in the still water of ponds and lakes or in the moving water of creeks and rivers. The fastest-growing area of interest in fly-fishing is salt water. Imagine a two-foot shark on a fly rod! Whether you live in the North or South, East or West, there are many fly-fishing opportunities you may not have even thought of, though you may have to be resourceful to find them.

Fly-fishing a river, or any moving water, generally involves changing conditions and situations.

Moving water: Rivers, streams, and creeks

Given my choice for a fly-fishing adventure, I head for the moving water of creeks, streams, or rivers. I enjoy the sound of running water, from a slight trickle dripping into a small pool to the deafening roar of a waterfall. The scene in a river is constantly changing because of the movement of the water. In any river or creek there are different kinds of water to fish, from one side of the river to the other, both upstream and down. There are shallow areas where the water runs faster and deeper pools where the water slows down. By learning to read the water, to identify the various types (see chapter 5), you will be able to find the places where fish are most likely to be. It's fun to try the different areas in a river, always looking to find where the fish are.

Fly-fishing a pond, or any still water, is somewhat more stable than fishing moving water, but it's just as enjoyable.

Still water: Ponds and lakes

You may not live near a trout stream, but don't feel you must limit your fly-fishing to that once-a-year vacation in the mountains. You don't need moving water; you can fly fish in a pond or lake. Fly-fishing in still water can be especially gratifying when the fish are feeding near the surface. You've probably seen those dimples on a lake, especially in the morning or evening when the water is calm. Those rings, called *rises*, are created by fish as they touch the surface of the water in order to eat insects. When the fish are rising, you actually have dinner-plate-sized targets at which to cast, each one made by a hungry fish.

Do you know of any parks in your area? Many parks have duck ponds that probably contain some kind of fish—and as someone once told me, "If it swims in the water, it can be caught on a fly rod." Bass, bluegill, sunfish, crappie, and even carp may all be waiting for you and your fly rod. Whether or not you've seen other fly fishers there, that pond is worth a try. Some of the largest fish live in the comfort of still water, and even a palm-sized sunfish can be great fun when it's pulling and jumping on the end of your line. I've often been tempted to sneak onto a golf course at dusk to find out exactly what lives in those water hazards. Once you start to fly fish, you will never look at any water the same way again!

I had the pleasure of meeting Barry Reynolds, coauthor of several books on fly-fishing for species other than trout (see chapter 10), and hearing him talk about what fun it can be to catch other species of fish. Although he lives in Colorado near all kinds of trout waters, he pursues fly-fishing for other species as an alternative to competing for sections of riverbank during the summer "combat fishing" months on so many rivers. He found that it was much more enjoyable and challenging to seek out new and different places, especially if it meant being the only fly fisher there and sometimes the only angler in certain areas of ponds and lakes. Barry had a slide show with pictures of himself and his friends (and his four-year-old son) catching everything from bluegill to pike and carp on a fly rod. (For what fly rods to use for which species, see the chart in chapter 6.)

When you are fishing in still water, you can work from the bank, or you can further your adventures by fishing from a boat, a canoe, or a float tube (see chapter 8). Watercraft will enable you to reach more water and to maneuver away from weeds or bushes where your fly can get hung up when you cast. If you fish from the shore, you might want to wear waders to keep your feet dry, but wading into a pond or lake is not always desirable, because your feet can get stuck in what I often refer to as "boot-sucking mud."

You can also fly fish from a dock, provided it's not too far above the water. In order to land a fish, you must lift it up out of the water, or be able to reach into the water to remove the fly. If you are fishing from a high dock or one with a rail, your leader might break before you are able to net or grab the fish.

Salt water

Saltwater fly-fishing is the fastest-growing area of the sport. As the coastal tide recedes from the shoreline, migrating and native fish come in to feed and are found in water that is sometimes only three feet deep. In many locations you can cast into the surf from the beach.

Fly-fishing in the surf or saltwater fishing from a boat can be fun and exciting because you never know what you're going to catch. One cast can produce a fish that looks long and skinny like an eel, and the next can bring in something that looks like a home aquarium angelfish. Fly fisher Nancy Wickes, 72, recounts her proudest accomplishment: landing a 100-pound sailfish on a fly rod in the Pacific off Costa Rica. And a week's fishing off the coast of Panama yielded 18 species of fish, all caught on different types of rods.

Gathering information

One of your best resources is a good map of your area. Get one out and start looking for any rivers or lakes. Also check your library for books about local fishing or outdoor recreation, including nearby parks. Many books about places to fish will have maps showing the surrounding area and access to water.

The people at your local fly shop should be your best resource for information. Have an idea about how far you'd be willing to travel, and then ask them about any places they'd recommend for your fishing adventure. Most shops keep current information about local fishing conditions and which flies and strategies have been successful.

The folks in the store can help you to select flies for your destination. If you have a fly box, bring it so they can see what flies you already have. Ask them about favorite spots and how to get to them. See if they have any maps of the area or if they will draw you a map. Most private property is marked, but they might save you some time by telling you specifically where to park and how to reach the water without trespassing.

If you are traveling to a place the shop owners are not familiar with, ask if they can recommend a fly shop there. You might want to wait to buy your flies at your destination, but it's always a good idea to have a basic fly assortment with you (see chapter 6) just in case you don't find a fly shop. People who operate fly-fishing businesses are a close-knit group, and many have a network of shops they recommend. If you can get a phone number, you might want to call ahead to find out what to expect about fishing conditions and the weather.

Destination books, such as Marty Bartholomew's *Flyfisher's Guide to Colorado*, are some of my favorite reading. Regional destination books are available from the West to the East Coast and include many places abroad (see chapter 10). In addition to specific information about access to fishing spots and what flies to use where, they often describe places to stay and list local fly shops to contact before or after you get there. As a rule, I always use a topographical map book or a good detailed local map in tandem with maps in those books to help keep my bearings and stay on course—usually—when I go exploring.

WHAT ELSE DO I NEED TO KNOW?

Fishing license

You will need a fishing license even if you don't catch or keep any fish. You can purchase a one-day, multiple-day, or annual license. The price will range from about $5 (one-day) to about $40 (annual). For details, contact your state's fish and game department, or division of wildlife (states have different names for the agency that regulates hunting and fishing). It usually costs less for state residents than for nonresidents.

Most states will have a handbook of fishing regulations. Perhaps only flies and artificial lures are legal for a particular stretch of water, or there may be restrictions on the size and number of fish that you can keep. You will need to know the opening and closing dates of each fishing season. And remember that if you cross into another state to fish, you will most likely need another license in order to be legal there too.

No trespassing

Watch for "no trespassing" and "no fishing" signs, and always ask for permission before fishing on private land. At worst, the owners will say "no." But sometimes you'll be pleasantly surprised at their willingness to let you fish on their property, especially if you practice catch-and-release fishing (see chapter 5) and offer to remove any trash you find. (Be sure, of course, to pack out your own.)

Chapter 4

BASIC TECHNIQUES

Left to right: These flies tied in **exacting patterns** imitate a mosquito, beetle, and grasshopper.

WHY IS CASTING SO IMPORTANT?

When you fly fish, you use artificially created or "tied" flies that are supposed to imitate real insects or water creatures. Flies are hand-tied from feathers, fur, and synthetic materials to resemble the mosquito that bites your arm, or the beetle that falls helplessly into the water. Some flies are tied to replicate exactly a specific insect, such as a grasshopper made to look like a real grasshopper in size and color; these flies are tied in *exacting patterns*. Other flies, tied in what are called *attractor patterns*, represent a variety of insects with similar profiles but do not duplicate real ones. You will never see a live insect that looks just like a Royal Wulff, its red body bracketed by green bands, or one with the iridescent, pearl-like body of the Flashback Pheasant Tail. But we hope to fool the fish into thinking that both exacting patterns and attractor patterns look good enough to eat.

Fish are constantly looking for naturally available or natural-appearing food sources. The flies we use to attract various kinds of fish range in size, shape, color, and behavior. Flies are

· ·

Becoming a good caster takes time, practice, and patience.

· ·

Flies come in different sizes for each pattern. Top left is a size #18 ant and at right is a size #8 ant.

referred to by their size and pattern name. Let's say we are using a red ant pattern. I can fish the ant in many different sizes. The size of the fly refers to the size of the hook on which it is tied: the smaller the number, the larger the fly. A size #8 red ant is almost twice as large as a size #18. (See hook size chart on page 37.)

Casting is the means of presenting a lure to the fish, and the way we cast flies is unique to fly-fishing. In spin-fishing, for example, the weight of the lure or a weight attached to the bait is snapped forward and travels through the air, pulling clear fishing line or monofilament behind it. In fly-fishing, however, the weight of the fly does not pull the line behind it but is itself pulled and pushed through the air by the weight and thickness of the fly line. The thick, plastic-coated colored line creates a loop that unfolds, presenting the leader with the fly at the end. The weighted fly line allows you to cast flies of very little weight to where you want them to go.

CASTING THEORY

A good cast is essential to fly-fishing. Many anglers believe that a cast is just a means to an end: they are pleased if the fly goes where they want it to, although the procedure isn't always pretty, and then the fishing begins. Others believe that casting is so important in itself that fly-fishing *is* casting. I believe that there is casting and then there is fishing, and that you'll be a much better angler if you develop the skills to do both.

One of the most frustrating things for beginners is not being able to get the fly where you want it to go or, worse, getting the line tangled or caught in something other than a fish's mouth. Becoming a good caster will help you overcome those challenges because you'll have more control over the line and the fly. I fly fished for many years with a horrible cast. Sometimes the fly would go right where I willed it, and I would catch fish. But all too often the fly would end up catching bushes and trees. If there was one blade of grass in the general area, it would be only a matter of time before I'd manage to hook it. At one point, I even thought about carrying garden shears with me so I could clear-cut an area free of "frustrations." Yet I stubbornly resisted listening to others who offered advice on how to improve my cast. Why? Aside from my injured pride, I can only conclude that the strength of my resistance depended on who was giving the tips. It seemed that the closer that person was to me—for instance, a blood relative or a loved one—the less able I was to heed the advice.

Seek help from an impartial party, preferably a professional who teaches casting and fly-fishing for a living. The more proficient you become at casting, the less frustrated you'll be, because you'll spend more time actually fishing than getting your fly out of the bushes and untangling your line. Don't be discouraged; increased skill will come with time and practice. Improving your cast is a lifelong pursuit. If you identify specific problems, or have reached a casting "plateau" where it seems you can't cast well beyond a certain distance, or you're not sure whether your technique is correct, there is nothing better than having a qualified instructor to get you over the hump. Most fly-fishing shops offer casting clinics, and some of their experts will even take time to work with you individually. Attending a fly-fishing school is another great way to get started. Practicing correct form and technique from the beginning can save you years of frustrating work.

A good cast consists of efficient use of energy and accurate placement or presentation of the fly. Think of the casting stroke as a transfer of energy or power. The energy travels from your arm, shoulder, and back muscles through your hand and wrist to the handle or butt of the rod, through the length of the rod and into the fly line, and is then transmitted through the leader, which ends with the fly.

You don't have to have a lot of upper-body or arm strength to cast. In fact, many instructors say that, in general, women make better casters than men when they are first learning. I think the reason is that women have a tendency to use more finesse in the casting stroke, rather than sheer muscle power. We have to "feel" the stroke instead of forcing it. There is power involved in casting, but the trick is to learn when to apply the power and when to let the rod do some of the work for us.

WHAT YOU NEED FOR CASTING PRACTICE

For casting practice, instead of a tied fly you'll be using only a piece of thick yarn without a hook, so you won't hook something you don't want to, including yourself. I recommend that you begin with an 8- to 9-foot rod for a 5- or 6-weight line because I think this setup is easier than other lengths and weights to start with. You will be able to feel this rod bending and working for you. And

EQUIPMENT FOR CASTING PRACTICE

- reel and 8- to 9-foot rod for a 5- or 6-weight line (on rod and line weight, see chapter 6)
- 7½-foot, 4X leader
- inch-long piece of gift-tying yarn
- glasses and hat for eye and face protection

To practice casting, tie a length of yarn onto the end of a leader so you can follow your cast.

I suggest a 7½-foot, 4X leader because this length is easier to cast than a 9- or 12-foot leader, and the 4X diameter at its end makes the leader less likely to break during practice than the thinner 5X or 6X. You can also use a thicker leader, such as a 2X or 3X, for practice. A used leader that has been cut back because of use or tangles will also work fine; just make sure it is at least 5 feet long, or it won't cast well.

Attach the leader to your fly line with a loop-to-loop connection (see chapter 3, page 35). You can practice casting on still water, but for your very first times it's best to practice on cut grass—a lawn or a mown park field—so that you can easily "unhook" your yarn if it should become stuck. (Avoid casting on asphalt or gravel, though, because the rough surface will damage the fly line.) Find a nice, open area, away from trees, bushes, and tall grass. Make sure you have plenty of room both in front and in back of you. The more line you are working with, the more space you'll need. I recommend that you wear sunglasses to protect your eyes from "stray line" and a hat with a brim for the same reason. These two items become essential when you are actually casting flies with hooks. (See page 86 on hook safety.)

String up your fly rod (see chapter 3) and pull at least three rod lengths of fly line, or about 20 to 25 feet through the end of the rod. Set the rod down, taking care not to step on it, and lay the line out in front of you on the ground in a straight line. (Except for this first exercise, you never want to lay your fly rod flat on the ground. Always stand it up against something like a picnic table or a tree, bush, or rock. It will be easier for you to find again, and, mainly, it won't get stepped on.)

On the end of your leader, attach a piece of gift-wrapping yarn. The yarn will not help your cast but will help you see where your cast is going. Make sure that the yarn is only about an inch long. A longer piece will be more difficult to cast because its larger mass will create more resistance in the air.

THE BASIC CAST

Stance

Casting stance with the foot on the side of your dominant hand slightly back for stability.

Take a comfortable stance with your feet about shoulder width apart, side by side. Once you decide which arm you'll cast with, move the foot on your *casting side* just slightly back to provide more stability.

Your shoulders should be facing forward, allowing you to face your target while you cast.

Grip

For the moment, hold your rod in your noncasting hand and drop your *casting arm* by your side. Bend your casting arm at the elbow, bringing the forearm up so that it is parallel to the ground. Extend your hand as if you are going to shake hands with someone. Now place the rod in your *casting hand*, grasping the handle with your thumb on top, allowing the reel to fall naturally below the palm side of your hand, under your wrist.

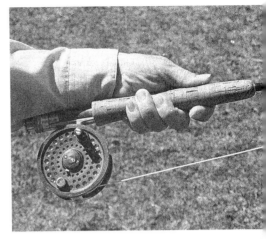

To grip the rod properly, place your thumb on top and allow the reel to fall below your wrist.

You may find that your hand becomes fatigued when you are first learning because you are holding the handle in a "death grip." If your fingers are turning white, your nails are digging into your palm, or your hand is cramping, put the rod in your noncasting hand for a moment while you shake and stretch out your casting hand. Over time, you'll know how hard you must grip the handle, and I have never seen a student cast away a fly rod because her grip was too loose!

Try the thumb on top first. If that isn't comfortable, you can try holding the handle with your index finger on top, or in the V between your thumb and index finger. Each of these grip styles has its devotees; however, when you begin to work on casting longer distances or learning different casting techniques, you will benefit most by using the thumb-on-top grip.

After you have the rod comfortably gripped in your casting hand, tuck the fly line under the index or middle finger of the same hand. Think of this finger as your contact with the line, which will come into play when we talk about ways to maintain tension and control while fishing. For now, pinching the line between your finger and the rod's grip will prevent more line from coming off the reel as you cast.

Students often ask at this point what to do with their noncasting hand. When you are first starting out, it can perch on your hip or rest comfortably at your side. Later, we will give this hand, known as your *line hand*, a task.

Motion

The casting motion consists of three basic parts: the *back cast*, the *stop* (or pause), and the *forward cast*. Before we start the actual casting instruction, keep in mind that the fly rod is designed to bend or flex. Many students are reluctant to let the rod bend for fear they will break it. But think for a moment about pole vaulting: the pole vaulter is shot through the air by the action of the pole bending. So don't be afraid to

Tuck the fly line under your index or middle finger for better line control.

apply the power that will cause the rod to flex during casting. Your fly line, just like the pole vaulter, will be "shot" through the air when your rod bends or *loads*.

The back cast

Start by holding your rod parallel to the ground, pointing forward. Imagine that you are standing beside a large clock face—your rod will point to 9 o'clock. Each practice cast will begin and end with the rod in this position.

Using power in the stroke, flip the rod up by bending your elbow in a quick motion, flinging the line up and behind you, and bringing the rod to a quick stop when it is pointing at 1 o'clock, or almost straight up at the sky. You should feel your forearm touch your biceps.

This is as far back as your rod and arm should go. The back-cast stroke is not a slow lifting motion but a quick, sharp flip with an abrupt stop. Imagine a grapefruit-sized ball of wet, heavy mud stuck on the end of your rod tip and try to fling the mud straight up and behind you. This quick, sharp motion or snap allows the rod to bend or flex, causing it to load.

The stop or pause

The second part of the cast, the stop, is easy: do nothing. Actually, while you do nothing, the rod is working for you by flipping the line into the air behind you. The abrupt stop, or pause, allows the line to travel back and straighten out, causing the rod to load, or bend backward. When you feel a slight tug or pull, then you are ready for your forward cast. The line must straighten out in the air behind you before you begin your front cast. Many beginners are reluctant to stop at this point, fear-

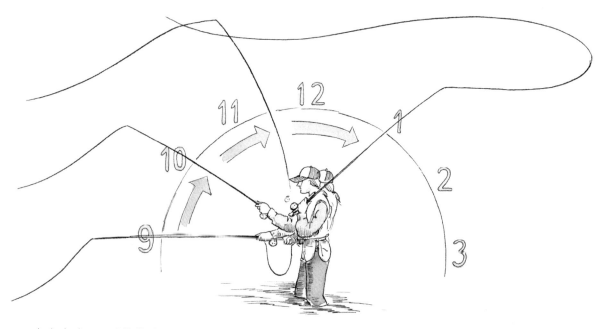

In the **back cast**, quickly flip the rod up from 9:00 to 1:00.

ing the line will fall to the ground. But the line will take longer to travel back than you might think. Remember, the more line you are casting, the longer time it needs to travel through the air, straighten out behind you, and then start forward. Shorter line casts need a shorter pause; longer line casts need a longer one.

The forward cast

If you have flipped the rod up with a power stroke and stopped the motion quickly with your rod pointing to 1 o'clock, you will feel a slight tug or pull during this pause as the line straightens out. The tug is your signal to begin the forward cast.

I think the forward cast may be the most difficult to master. It seems simple enough to think of just bringing the rod from the 1 o'clock position back down to 9 o'clock, parallel to the ground, but there are some challenges. You apply power in the forward stroke, but the key is

A tight loop will cut through the air more easily and efficiently than a wide loop.

wide open

tight loop

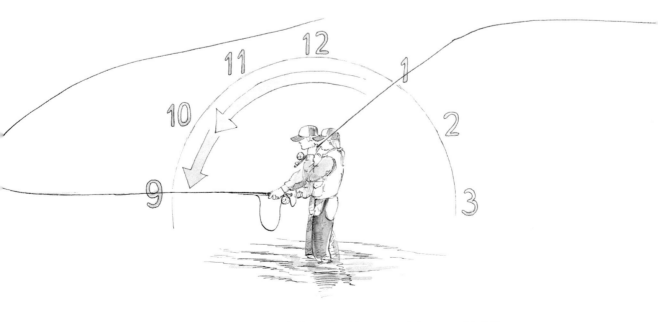

Bring your **forward cast** down from 1:00, snapping your wrist forward and down as you bring your rod to 9:00.

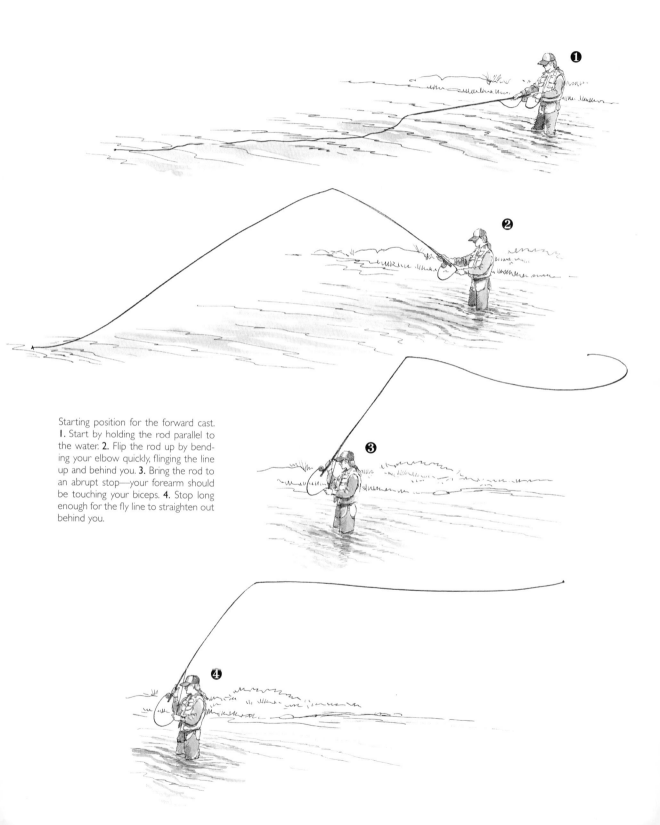

Starting position for the forward cast. **1.** Start by holding the rod parallel to the water. **2.** Flip the rod up by bending your elbow quickly, flinging the line up and behind you. **3.** Bring the rod to an abrupt stop—your forearm should be touching your biceps. **4.** Stop long enough for the fly line to straighten out behind you.

5. You'll feel the rod bend backward. 6. Begin the forward cast. 7. Snap your wrist forward as you drive your arm forward and down. 8. Follow through until both rod and arm are parallel to the water.

Extending your arm in the forward cast (top) will reduce the power of your cast. Arm in correct position for forward cast (right).

when to apply it. With the rod in the 1 o'clock position, as the line straightens out above and behind you, it actually comes to a stop. The forward cast must bring the rod forward and down slowly at first to get the line momentum going forward. Then, when the rod is at about 11 o'clock, snap your wrist over forward by rolling it and pressing your thumb forward, at the same time bringing your forearm parallel to the ground again.

This sequence of events will cause the line to roll forward and create a loop or U shape. If you use all wrist and no arm motion, the loop will be too open. A combination of arm and wrist motions give you what we call a *tight loop*. A tight loop is better because its torpedo shape cuts through the air more easily and gives you more control over where the line is going. This is especially true in windy conditions, or when you begin to cast more line.

In the forward cast, the wrist bends forward, then, the arm drives forward and down toward the ground, and the rod and arm stop at 9 o'clock, parallel to the ground. Be careful not to let your upper arm extend away from your body, as you will lose power. Pick a target, such as a leaf, flower, or rock, and try to get your yarn fly to land there. Estimating distance will come with time.

One more thing: in a good cast, the line lands in a straight line, and its whole length touches down at about the same time. Keep in mind that when you are casting on water, you want the fly line to straighten out at almost the same time as it touches the water. If you bring your forward cast down too hard and low, the line will slap the water, causing you to scare or *line* the fish.

TROUBLESHOOTING

Oh, how I wished when I was starting out that I had a casting doctor! It would have been so easy simply to pick up the phone, call the doctor, explain the symptoms of my poor, ill-looking cast, and receive immediate feedback on how to fix the problem. Now, one of my favorite parts of a teaching class consists of "diagnosing the symptoms" of casting problems. When you are first learning, you will probably encounter some of the common ones. Not to worry. You are not alone in these troubles—believe me, I've been there! This whole casting procedure sounds simple enough, but I bet every beginner had similar difficulties. Here is a list of common symptoms with some recommendations for remedies.

- **"I don't feel the tug or pull of the fly line at the end of my back cast."** Try really flipping or popping the line up off the grass or water. You may not be giving the back cast enough power to load the rod. Don't baby the rod. With a quick, sharp motion, bring the rod up to 1 o'clock by bending at your elbow, not your wrist. Think of a quick acceleration to a quick and sharp stop.

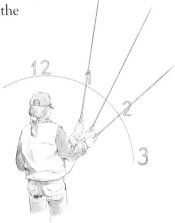

- **"I am afraid the line is going to come right at my face."** As soon as the line starts moving in the grass, give it a quick snap of energy. The line can come right at your face in the back cast only if you slowly lift or drag it instead of flipping it with energy and power. You might also try tilting your forearm slightly away from your shoulder, approaching a sidearm motion (see right).

Tilt forearm slightly away from your shoulder to keep the line away from your face.

- **"I hear a snapping sound behind me"** or **"My line is falling to the ground in front of me like a pile of spaghetti."** To prevent either from happening, try pausing or stopping longer after you make your back cast. The snap you hear, much like the cracking of a wet towel when you snap it at someone, is actually the line doubling back on itself. Hesitate a little longer than you think you need to—sometimes it helps to count slowly, "one, two"—before you begin your forward cast. It may seem like an eternity of waiting, but you really have more time than you think before the line will fall to the ground.

Choose a **casting plane** that's comfortable for your arm. Rod travels back and forth close to shoulder (**A**). Rod travels farther away from your face (**B**). A more side-arm plane casts line more easily under trees (**C**). Cast in a plane across your body to keep line away from bushes (**D**).

Top: You can't cast effectively with an **open wrist**, with space between the rod and your forearm. **Above:** A **closed wrist**, with the rod close to or against your forearm, allows you more power and better control of the rod.

- **"I am catching the ground behind me."** Either your pause after the back cast is too long or more likely, you are letting your wrist roll too far back during the back cast, bringing the rod to the 2 or 3 o'clock position. Think of stopping the rod and your thumb so that both point almost straight up, no farther back than 1 o'clock.

- **"I don't see a loop in my line on the forward cast."** Try looking at your wrist the entire time while you are casting. It is likely that you are bending only with your wrist and not using enough or any elbow. Try a few casts where you look at your line. Then try a few more where you watch your wrist. Think about keeping the end or butt of the rod fairly close to or almost touching your forearm during your back cast. The loop, you remember, is created in the forward cast by pushing down with your thumb, pivoting your wrist forward and down, so that the loop shoots directly toward your target.

- **"The line is hitting itself or the rod during the front cast."** Try to keep your rod tip traveling in the same plane while you are making your back cast and your forward cast. Follow through with an application of power by pivoting your wrist and pressing down toward the ground with your thumb, almost at the end of your forward cast.

These are only a few of the troubles you may have when you are working on your cast. Becoming a good caster takes time, practice, and patience. You've heard the saying that "practice makes perfect." What they don't usually tell you is that only *perfect* practice makes perfect! Not to worry though. Everyone makes casting mistakes when starting out. In fact, what you spend time working on while casting on dry land may go right out the window when you actually get to the water. The main thing is to try not to get so involved with thinking about casting that you are reluctant to go out fishing. Your casting skills will increase with time. If you are having a lot of difficulty on your own, you may want to consider taking a class, or finding

WALKING WITH A FLY ROD IN HAND

Keeping tension on your fly line is the key to keeping your line under control when you are walking from one point to another. Leaving the line or fly loose will allow it to get hooked in bushes. The best thing to do is to latch the fly to the hook keeper and wind any slack line onto the reel. Although this may seem a tedious process, it'll help you to manage your line in the long run. If you don't have a fly to latch onto the hook keeper, grasp the leader under the handle where you are holding the fly rod.

When walking with your fly rod, if you don't have a fly attached to your leader, grasp the leader under the handle to maintain control of the line.

After you have the line under control, you can walk with either your rod tip or the butt end forward. In thick brush I prefer to walk with the butt end forward to avoid getting the tip hooked up in the brush. This way, the tip trails behind my shoulder (though you must use care, if others are following you, not to poke them in the face with your rod!). In more open areas I prefer to walk with the tip end forward, as the rod feels more comfortable and balanced in my hand. I often let my noncasting hand carry the rod in order to give my casting hand and arm a rest.

a qualified instructor. But try not to be like one woman who came to a class, and all she wanted to do was learn to cast, cast, cast. By the end of the lessons, she was a beautiful caster, but as she admitted herself, she had little interest in actually fishing. As I mentioned, I view the cast as just one part of the fly-fishing process. It is also important that you learn what to do *after* you make that beautiful cast and put the fly where you want it.

MORE ADVANCED CASTING CONCEPTS

Shooting or extending line

The basic cast would work well all day long if you were using exactly the same amount of line each time. But the amount of line you need will sometimes change. You must then learn how to get more line out. After you feel somewhat comfortable with the basic casting stroke, you are ready to practice *shooting line*. Here's where your noncasting or line hand finally gets a task.

Make a basic cast. After the line is lying still, begin to pull it off the grass or water with your

Hand positions for **stripping line in.**

. . . .

Shooting line is all in the timing: it's about knowing when to let go.

. . . .

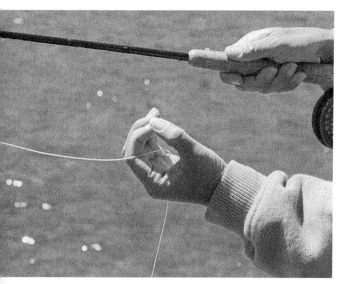

Near the end of your forward cast, **shoot the line** by forming an O between the thumb and fingers of your line hand and allow the line to slide through it.

line hand working in between the reel and your rod hand. This is known as *stripping line in.* Strip in a 12- to 18-inch-section at a time, letting the line glide over the index or middle finger of your rod hand, until you have pulled in about 10 to 12 feet. Let this line lie by your feet. Now, with your line hand, reach up to the stripping guide and pinch the line between the index finger and thumb. Then, still pinching the line, drop your noncasting hand down by your belly button and let go of the line with your casting hand. Pinching the line very tightly in your line hand, make a few casts, holding the line the entire time. You will feel a series of tugs on your line hand while you are casting. On the last tug, when your rod is in about the 10 o'clock position in your forward cast, make your line hand form a circle or a trough and let the line slide through it.

Shooting line is all in the timing: it's about knowing when to let go. It is important to pinch the line tightly throughout the cast until you are ready to release it near the end of your forward cast. Your mind will say, "now!" and I want you to wait for just a second and then let go. More often than not, you will want to shoot too early. Remember that releasing the line to shoot it is almost the last thing you do in the cast.

After the line is cast out, your noncasting hand will hand the line off to the middle or index finger of your casting hand, and the process of stripping line in begins again. You can extend a short section of line, a section at a time, or shoot the whole thing. Make a habit of good line-handling skills. Either your line hand or one finger of your rod hand needs to be in contact with the fly line so that at any time you can raise your rod to put tension on

• •

Before you practice false casting, it is important that you first feel comfortable with the basic three-step cast. Shooting line and false casting are just maneuvers that build on the basic casting stroke.

• •

the line. Think about being able to move the fly line with your rod at any time. This tension plays an important part in hooking, playing, and landing a fish.

False casting

False casting is a term we use for a series of back and forward casts during which the fly line never touches the ground or water, but is cast to and fro in the air several times before it is set down on the water. False casting is fluid and graceful, almost artistic looking. If you have ever watched anyone fly-fishing, you have probably seen it done.

False casts are beneficial to fly fishers for several reasons. When a fly that is designed to float absorbs water and begins to sink under the surface, false casting allows the angler to flip it back and forth through the air, giving it a chance to dry before putting it back on the water.

False casting is also used when you would like to move the line to another location. For instance, if the river current has carried your fly and line too far downstream, a series of false casts can maneuver them back upstream. By using a false cast, you can also extend line while casting.

Before you practice false casting, it is important that you first feel comfortable with the basic three-step cast. Shooting line and false casting are just maneuvers that build on the basic casting stroke. To work on false casting, start again with only about 25 feet of line. Make a basic cast and let the line lie out in front of you on the grass. Pinch the line against the cork grip with a finger of your casting hand to maintain control, not allowing more line to be pulled off the reel during your cast.

Next, just as in your basic cast, begin with your rod in the 9 o'clock position and use your power stroke to flip the line quickly, with an abrupt stop at 1 o'clock. Pause long enough to let the line straighten out behind you, but then bring your forward cast to 10 o'clock only and stop the rod again, allowing the line to straighten out in

Use a roll cast when obstacles such as bushes don't leave you enough room for a backcast.

the air in front of you. (Now you can finally see what your line has been doing behind you in your basic cast.) The line should not touch or slap the ground. As you see it begin to straighten, flip the rod back to 1 o'clock and pause again. Now bring the rod back down to 9 o'clock to complete a four-part series of strokes.

Remember that you need to pause for the same amount of time in the front cast as you do in your back cast. The tendency is to allow too short a pause in your back cast. I try to think of counting to a cadence to help me time both the front and the back stops in false casts. I flip the line back to 1 o'clock and count, "one, two, three," then cast the line forward—stopping at 10 o'clock—and count "one, two, three," back again to 1 o'clock and count "one, two, three," then the rod comes down to 9 o'clock.

When you are first starting out, limit your false casts to four or, at the most, six strokes. As you begin to become more comfortable with the timing, you can increase the number, but don't get carried away. The more false casts in your series, the more your timing in the front and back casts must be just right, or the line will lose power and the cast will collapse. Use only what you need to accomplish your purpose in false casting. When you are fishing, after all, you want to maximize the time that your line and fly are on the water, and minimize the time they are in the air.

False casting and extending line

This next technique often reminds me of learning to pat your head and rub your tummy. We are going to put it all together by combining the casting techniques you've learned so far. Once you're comfortable with performing a series of false casts, you can extend line in the air as do them.

To begin, start with about 35 feet of fly line laid out on the grass in front of you. Just as when you practiced shooting line, strip an 8- to 10-foot length of line by pulling the line under your index or middle finger and letting it collect by your feet. Reach toward the stripping guide with your line hand and tightly pinch the line between the thumb and index finger. Remember to keep pinching tightly or you will lose line control. Begin your false cast with your power stroke, flipping the rod back and stopping at 1 o'clock. As you bring the rod forward in your front false cast, form an O with the thumb and index finger of your line hand, and let line shoot forward into your front cast during your pause at 10 o'clock. As your forward cast straightens out, tightly pinch the line with your casting hand while bringing the rod back to 1 o'clock. Pause, then bring the rod down to the 9 o'clock position and shoot the rest of the line. To maintain good line control, you should shoot or release line only in your forward cast.

After all the line is extended, repeat the whole process over again, beginning with stripping back in 8 to 10 feet of line. As tedious as this process may seem, it will soon become almost second nature to you, and you won't even think about the steps involved, you'll just do them. This false-casting and extending-line series is a fundamental you need to learn. You can use the technique right after you string up your rod to extend the line you need in order to begin fishing. There will also be many times while fishing that you'll repeatedly strip line in and then cast it out again.

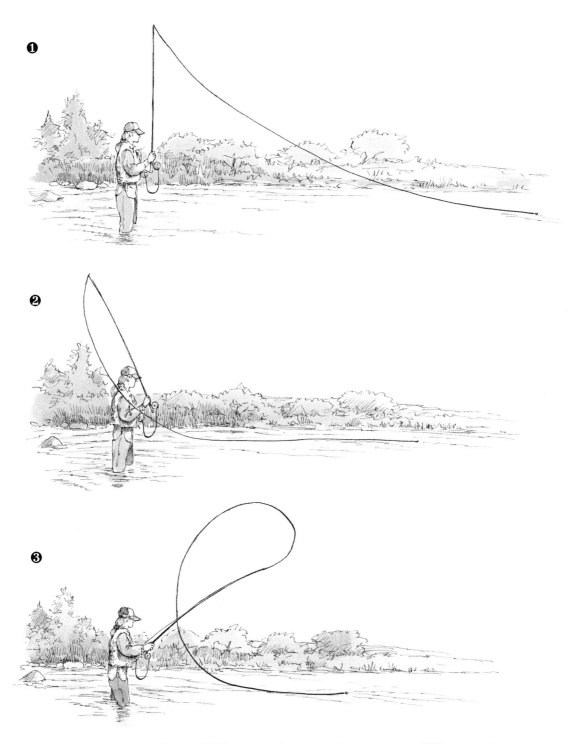

In the roll cast, slowly bring the rod back to 1:00 **(1)**, leaving the line touching the water, and pause **(2)**. Then, punch the rod down toward the water as you drop your elbow **(3)**.

Roll cast

A *roll cast* is a cast without a full back cast. It consists almost entirely of a forward casting motion. A roll cast is very useful when obstacles such as bushes behind you don't leave you enough room for a back cast. The roll cast must be practiced on water because it's the resistance of the line on the surface of the water that enables the rod to load or bend, giving you power and direction in your cast.

Begin with your line in the water in front of you. The stance and grip are the same as for your basic cast. Slowly raise your rod by bending your elbow, bringing the rod to the 1 o'clock position (as at the end of a back cast). The difference is that you leave the line touching the water. After you raise your rod, pause for a moment and let the line stop moving toward you on the water. (You can actually wait for several minutes with the line in this position.) Then, with your line still on the water and your rod pointing up to 1 o'clock, quickly, using a power stroke, punch your rod down to 9 o'clock as you drop your elbow. Your wrist should snap forward, when the rod is at about 11 o'clock, in the same manner it does in the basic forward cast. Your line should create a circle or loop in front of you as it travels forward. With practice, you will be able to roll cast at least 20 to 30 feet of line.

If you have difficulty gaining confidence in these skills, the best advice I can give you is to work with a qualified instructor. Nothing can take the place of spending time with someone who can teach you good fundamentals. I have never worked with anyone who wasn't able to learn how to cast. (For additional techniques and casts, see the recommended reading in chapter 10.)

Chapter 5

ADVANCED TECHNIQUES

FROM THE FLY LINE TO THE FLY

During my first fly-fishing experiences, I remember having to rely on the patience of my dad and brother to tie my knots for me. I had been a Girl Scout, for goodness' sake, and yet there I was trudging up and down the river, looking for a man of the family to tie on my flies. One of the best fishing gifts

The goal is to achieve a sneaky presentation so that when the fly lands in the water it seems to float freely and unencumbered.

my dad ever gave me was a waterproof knot booklet that I could keep in my vest (see chapter 10). With that book, I was suddenly emancipated! I was free to be on my own, and I remember how good it felt to be more independent. Even if you never fish alone, you should be able to do things for yourself, especially rigging up your own line. As Suzanne Mingo, 50, advises, even though she usually fishes with her husband, "learn your knots and learn to be self-sufficient when you are fishing."

Before learning how to tie knots, you should know the how and why of your line system, from the inside of the reel down to the fly. A typical line setup for fly-fishing, starting from the *arbor* or center post of the reel, includes backing, line, butt section, leader, tippet, and fly. The whole setup is stored on your reel, so at the end of your fishing day you simply cut off your fly

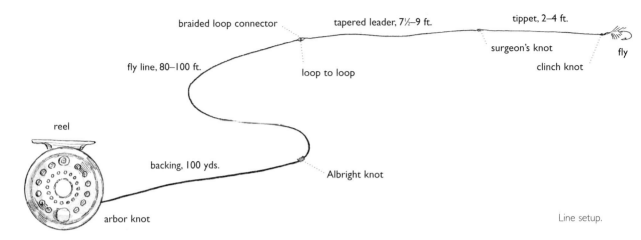

braided loop connector

tapered leader, 7½–9 ft.

tippet, 2–4 ft.

fly line, 80–100 ft.

surgeon's knot

fly

loop to loop

clinch knot

reel

backing, 100 yds.

Albright knot

arbor knot

Line setup.

(return it to your fly box to use again) and reel in everything else, including the fly line, leader, and tippet.

Backing

Backing is the material that is tied directly to the arbor of the reel. It's made of braided Dacron and looks like unwaxed dental floss. It comes in different colors, including orange and fluorescent yellow, though white is the most common. A typical trout setup has 100 yards of backing, wound on the reel first, before anything else. The fly line is then tied to the backing.

Backing serves to fill the reel, allowing the fly line to be coiled less tightly around the arbor. Tight coils would lie on the water in curlicues instead of a straight line. Some anglers also refer to the backing as an "insurance policy": if your fish heads downstream or across the lake, it can swim that extra 100 yards away from you and still be connected to your line. Backing is relatively inexpensive material, costing about $6 to $7.50 per 100 yards.

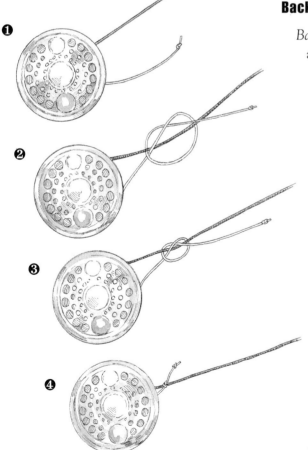

❶

❷

❸

❹

The **arbor knot** connects the fly backing to the reel. **1.** Wrap backing around the reel arbor and tie an overhand knot in the tag end. **2.** Take the short end and wrap an overhand knot around the line (long) end. **3.** Pull on tag end to tighten the overhand knot. **4.** Pull line end until the knot slides down the line to the arbor.

Fly line

Plastic-coated fly line ranges in color from bright orange and fluorescent yellow to pale yellow or gray. A fly line is usually 90 feet in length and has a taper to it. Fly lines that float, sink, or have just a tip that sinks (called *sink tip lines*) are made for different fishing situations, usually depending on how deep you want to fish your flies. The most common line for fly-fishing is a *floating line* because with it you can fish flies either on the surface of the water or, simply by adding weight onto your leader, underneath the water. Fly lines range in price from around $20 to $60. The more expensive lines are longer (up to 105 feet) and have special features, such as a slick finish to make casting and shooting line easier. Fly lines come in different thicknesses or weights, designed to match the type or weight of your rod (see chapter 6).

Butt section

Attached to the fly line is the butt section, which serves as a transition between line and leader. The leader *can* be tied directly to the fly line, but I don't recommend it, because every time you change your leader, you'll lose a bit of fly line with each new knot. In order to save the length and taper of your fly line, I advise you to use a butt section. There are two main types: a 3-inch braided loop and a 12- to 36-inch length of heavy monofilament.

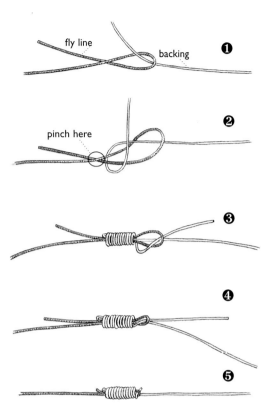

Use the **Albright** knot to tie fly line to the backing. **1.** Insert the backing through a loop in the fly line, allowing 8–10 inches on the tag end of the backing. **2.** Pinch together the two strands of the loop and the backing, and run the backing over all three strands. **3.** Using your left hand to control the wraps, wrap the tag end of the backing around the looped fly line and the backing, making about ten wraps. **4.** Insert the tag end of the backing through the loop in the fly line, catching the end of the backing. **5.** Pull taut. **6.** Clip ends of both lines close to the wrap.

Leaders

Leaders are lengths of clear, tapered material ranging from 6 feet to 16 feet long. They come in packages that look like envelopes and range in cost from $3.50 to $6.50. Leaders are made from different materials, the lower-cost ones usually of nylon and the more expensive leaders of material called fluorocarbon, which is relatively new to the market.

Fluorocarbon material is less visible in the water than nylon because the way it refracts light makes it nearly invisible to fish; however, the trade-off is that fluorocarbon is not as strong as nylon of the same diameter. Fluorocarbon leaders are designed to break the surface tension of the water and therefore sink, which is great if you are just fishing with flies subsurface. I do not recommend them for dry-fly-fishing, though, since the material will sink and have a tendency to pull

Leader kits come in many forms, but all contain a variety of lengths and tapers.

your floating flies underwater. Nylon leaders float on the surface of the water, unless you attach a weight or weighted fly on the end, causing it to sink. Nylon leaders are therefore more versatile, since you can use them both for dry flies on the surface and for flies fished underwater.

There are *knotless* and *knotted* leaders. The more common knotless leader is one continuous strand of material, thick where it is attached to the butt section and gradually tapering to the thin end where you will attach your fly. This tapering system, from the thick and heavy fly line to the thin and weightless end of the leader, is what allows you to cast the fly to land in the water looking like the real thing.

Knotted leaders are also tapered but are made by tying differing thicknesses of material together: a thick piece is tied to a finer piece, and so on, with the finest piece on the end to which you tie your fly. Before a process was developed to taper one continuous length of material, all leaders were tied in this manner, by hand. You can buy knotted leaders, or you can construct your own by purchasing a *leader kit*, which contains many spools of material in various diameters to make a few dozen leaders. Most leader kits come with instructions telling you how long to cut each piece of the leader and what knots to use. A leader kit costs about $45. Some anglers tie their own leaders because doing so can save them money or because they think a knotted leader is easier to cast. But I've found that the knotted connections have a tendency to pick up pieces of moss in the water, so I favor a knotless leader for most fishing situations.

Keep in mind that all leader material has a shelf life of only two or three years. Over time, it will lose its elasticity and become brittle, especially if it's left in direct sunlight. You should never, for instance, leave leader packages on the dashboard of a car. If you can't remember how old your leaders are, it's probably a good idea to replace them. In fact, it's a better idea to use new leaders for every fishing season.

Leaders taper to different thicknesses at the end, each designated by a number followed by an X, such as 4X or 5X. To feel the taper, take the leader out of its package and pull it between your fingers, starting with the heavy end. The X number refers to the diameter of the fine end: the larger the number, the thinner the end. How fine a leader to use depends on the size of the fly you choose and whether you want to fish in the fast water of a river or the calm, clear water of a lake.

It would be a lot more simple if we could attach the fly right on the end of the colored fly line. But imagine how that would look to the fish. The fly would land with a splat on the water and appear to be attached to

Use the lengths I give only as a guideline: there are no absolute rules for matching length of leader to a situation.

a piece of stiff, colored piano wire. Tapering allows the power in the cast to be transmitted and diffused from the rod to the fly line to the almost invisible leader, which finally directs the fly. The goal of the cast and the line setup is to make the fly appear natural to the fish. The smaller the fly, the thinner the leader should be to make it appear lifelike—attached to, for instance, spider webs, not piano wire.

Fly Size to Leader Taper

Leader or Tippet Size	Diameter, inch	Approximate Strength, pounds	Appropriate Fly Sizes
0X	0.011	15.5	1/0, 2
1X	0.010	13.5	4, 6, 8
2X	0.009	11.5	6, 8, 10
3X	0.008	8.5	10, 12, 14
4X	0.007	6.0	12, 14, 16
5X	0.006	4.75	14, 16, 18
6X	0.005	3.5	16, 18, 20, 22
7X	0.004	2.5	18, 20, 22, 24
8X	0.003	1.75	22, 24, 26, 28

A 6X leader has a finer end than a 3X leader and is thus more nearly invisible in the water. The finer the leader, however, the weaker it becomes, so you always want to use the thickest material you can get away with. For example, according to the chart, to fish with a fly size #14 you could tie it to either 3X, 4X, or 5X material. How to decide? In faster, more turbulent water, where a fish has little time to examine the fly, you'd probably want to use 3X. The thicker and stronger material would also give you a better chance to hold your fish on the line in heavy current. In contrast, in a very still, clear pool or lake you could best fool the fish by using 5X, the thinnest leader listed for your #14 fly, so that it would not appear to be tied to anything.

The length of the leader you choose has to do with what and where you are fishing and in what sort of water. Leaders come in lengths from 6 feet all the way up to 16 feet—most commonly 7½ and 9 feet. The longer the leader, the more difficult it is to cast, but you can't always get away with a short one. Let's say you come across a deep, quiet pool in a river, and toward the end of the pool (the *tail out*), you see a fish cruising for food. You'd want to use a longer leader, perhaps 9 or 12 feet, because the water is so still and calm. You would also probably want to use a 9-foot leader if you were fishing sinking flies in a river with deeper water, because the longer length will help you get your flies down deep. In moving and churning water, however, you can get away with a shorter leader, probably 7½ feet.

Use these lengths only as a guideline. There are no absolute rules for matching length of leader to a situation. Sometimes fish will take a fly on a very short leader; at other times you may fool them better with a longer one. Fly-fishing requires adaptation and experimentation.

Tippet

Tippet is monofilament material that you tie to the end of your leader. Whereas leaders come in different lengths and are tapered, tippet comes on spools (usually 30 meters per spool) and is the same diameter throughout its entire length.

Tippet is used for several different reasons. You now know that a leader tapers in diameter from the thick end to the fine end to which you attach your fly. Let's suppose you want to fish with a size #14 fly on a clear pond, and you select a 9-foot, 5X leader. Starting out, you can tie your #14 fly right onto the leader. But as you begin to fish, say you get your fly stuck on a bush, and it breaks off. Suppose you tie on another #14 fly and continue to fish. Then perhaps you get a fish on the line and the leader breaks—and you lose the fly and the fish. By now you've lost a foot or so of your 9-foot leader, and the end of it isn't 5X in diameter anymore. Your leader is now only 8 feet, ending in 4X material. At this point you have two options. You can throw the shortened leader in the trash and start again with a new 5X leader in order to fish your #14 sized fly, or you can tie on about a 12-inch piece of 5X tippet material to restore both the leader's 9-foot length and its original 5X taper. A leader might cost about $3.50. A 30-meter spool of tippet material will also cost $3.50. You save money by having tippet material on hand instead of using up so many leaders.

Tippet allows you to be more versatile. For instance, by adding tippet you can lengthen a 7½-foot leader when you need to. It also lets you use more sizes of flies. On 5X material you can fish sizes #14, #16, and #18 flies. But if you tie on a piece of tippet that is one X finer, such as 6X tippet on a 5X leader, you can also fish fly sizes #20 and #22. You always want to tie on only tippet of the same diameter as the leader or one X finer. If you tie 7X tippet on a 5X leader, the knot may hold, but the line leading up to the fly will not have the gradual taper you need to cast it more effectively. Nor should you add thicker material onto thinner material. Tying a piece of 4X onto a 5X leader, for instance, would also destroy the gradual tapering system.

If you don't know how long or thick a leader is, estimate its length by measuring out one-foot sections, counting aloud "one, two, three" until you reach the other end. It's OK to approximate here. When you have figured its length—say, 6 feet—you can then compare the thinner end of the leader with different spools of tippet, holding the two together to compare diameters, looking and feeling the material to find the closest match. If you conclude that the closest match to the end of your leader is 4X tippet, you know that you can attach a 15- to 18-inch section of either 4X or 5X tippet to make a 7½-foot, 4X or 5X leader.

KNOTS

There are only three basic knots you should know by heart: the *perfection loop*, the *double overhand* or *surgeon's knot*, and the *clinch knot*. You'll be using the latter two almost all the time.

But first, there are some general things to remember when tying all knots. Before tightening the knots down, the monofilament should be moistened either with your mouth or by dipping the material in the water. Moistening the knots will reduce the amount of friction that occurs when the material rubs against itself in being tightened. Even the slightest friction weakens the material. Moistening will also lubricate the material, allowing the knots to be pulled tight.

Another thing to keep in mind is the right way to tighten these knots. I've noticed when I'm teaching knot-tying clinics that students often tend to snap or "bounce" their knots tight to test whether they are going to hold. Try instead to tighten your knots with slow, gradual, increasing pressure until you feel a slight stretch in the material, especially when working with leader and tippets of very thin diameter. I always hold the piece I'm adding to the system in my dominant hand, because it's smarter and can manipulate the material more easily than my nondominant hand, which can do things like grasp and pinch.

It may take you a few tries to tie these knots well, so don't use your brand new fly line and leaders to practice! Practice first with dental floss. Then, when you feel confident enough to try the real thing, start with thicker-diameter tippet such as 2X or 3X and gradually work your way down to finer leaders and tippets of 5, 6, and 7X. You may not be able to fish whenever you want to, but you can always find time to practice your knots.

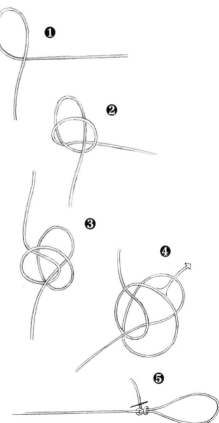

- **Perfection loop.** This knot is formed both at the end of your butt section and at the thick end of your leader. (Some fly lines and leaders come with a loop already attached at the end, but learn this knot anyway in case you need to repair your line during fishing.) The two loops are then joined in a loop-to-loop connection.

  The end of the line that will eventually be cut off we can call the *tag end*. The rest of the line we'll call the *line end*. Start by pinching your practice fly line in your nondominant hand with your thumb and forefinger, allowing at least 6 inches of tag end to come out from behind your thumb. Take your tag end and form a loop with the tag end in back of the line end (1). Wrap the tag end around the line end and pinch the tag in back of your loop. Gently pull on this second loop you've just created, making it stand up. The remaining tag end should be sticking out in the same direction as when you

Tie a **perfection loop** onto the end of a leader to attach the leader to the loop on the fly line.

I always hold the piece I'm adding to the system in my dominant hand, because it's smarter and can manipulate the material more easily than my nondominant hand, which can do things like grasp and pinch.

started (2). Lay the tag end between the two loops (3). From the back, reach through the first loop, grab the second loop, and pull it through the first. As the knot begins to tighten, keep pulling on the loop while letting everything else go except the line itself (4). Pull tight. If tied correctly, the loop should not pull out like a slip knot. I usually put a pen or hemostat through the loop and tighten by pulling on first the line end and then the tag end. This is the only knot I cut flush: that is, without leaving any tag end (5).

- **Loop-to-loop connection.** Once you have a loop in the butt section or the end of your fly line and a loop on the end of your leader, you are ready to join the two (see illustration on page 69). Insert the fly line loop through the leader loop. Double over the heavy end of your leader, about two inches away from the leader loop, and push this material through the fly line loop. Pull the leader all the way through. The loop-to-loop connection may not look tight, and you might see some play in it. But even if it appears loose, this connection will come apart only if you push the leader back out through the fly line loop. This joining method makes changing leaders very easy.

- **Double overhand or surgeon's knot.** This knot joins tippet to leader. You will be attaching 12 to 36 inches of tippet to your leader, depending on the situation. Always give yourself plenty of material to work with, and you will find these knots less frustrating to tie; you can always trim off the excess. (When you are practicing, you can tie tippet to tippet in order to save your leaders for fishing.)

    Pinch your leader between the thumb and forefinger of your nondominant hand. Pinch your tippet between the thumb and

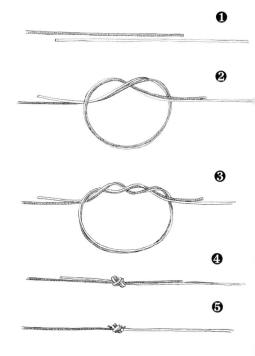

❶

❷

❸

❹

❺

The **double overhand** or **surgeon's knot** is used to tie the leader to the tippet.

forefinger of your other hand. Overlap these two about 4 inches, again pinching the material with your thumbs and forefingers (1). Make a loop in the 4-inch section of overlap,

● ●

Knots are the weakest link in the entire system. Take the time to make sure yours are tied well.

● ●

and pinch the cross between the thumb and forefinger of your nondominant hand. Using your dominant hand, wrap the long and the short ends on that side through the loop (2). (You can wrap either direction as long as you continue to wrap the ends in the same direction.) Wrap the long and the short end—the same ones—again through the loop (3). Moisten the wraps. Pull all four ends and gradually tighten the knot (4). Don't bounce it. Instead, apply a slow, gradual pressure. Release the short ends and pull on the long ends. Finish tightening by pulling on all four ends to turn. To complete the knot, trim the short ends to about ⅟₁₆ inch (5).

- • **Clinch knot.** You will use this knot (see page 38) to tie your fly to the end of your leader or tippet. Of all the knots, you will use the clinch knot the most, and I recommend that you practice it until you know it very well.

I always test the knots I've tied by pulling on them with gradual pressure. If tied well, they will take quite a bit of pressure. I would rather have my knots come apart in my hands than during a fight with a fish. If you tie a knot that doesn't look quite right, or you aren't sure you've tied it correctly, tie it again. Knots are the weakest link in the entire system. Take the time to make sure yours are tied well.

FLY-FISHING STRATEGY

Reading moving water: rivers, streams, and creeks

A friend and new fly fisher recently asked me, "when you get to a river you've never fished before and you know nothing about it, what do you look for to find where the fish are holding?" Fish are more likely to be in some places than others. They need shelter, food, and a water temperature that is comfortable for them. When these basic needs are met, they have no reason to move elsewhere. In many places, however, fish migrate up rivers or into channels in search of one or more of those needs.

Assuming that the water we're talking about is a suitable place for our fish to live, finding out where they are is part of the adventure of fly-fishing. I like to compare myself to the hawks and kingfishers I see, and laugh at the thought that we are all out there looking for fish together. One of my fishing buddies told me that when he was once fishing a deep pool in the winter, an eagle swooped down and flew away with the large trout he was trying to catch!

Persistence usually,
though not always,
pays off with this sport.

Smaller streams or creeks tend to be easier to read than larger ones, but don't let the size of a river overwhelm you. You only can fish one side of a river at a time anyway, so instead of letting big water confuse you, imagine it divided into smaller parts, and look for structure and signs only in the parts you can access.

Riffles, pools, and runs

Rivers are defined by certain characteristics of water. The more you know about a stream's structure by observing its different kinds of water, the better you will be able to fish. Under various conditions, fish will more often be found in one type of water than another.

Riffles are fairly fast, shallow sections of water. Fish will feed in riffles from late spring through fall, when the warmer water temperature makes the fish more active. Fish holding in riffles are hungry and thus easier to catch; however, it's more difficult to see them in riffles because the water is so busy.

Pools are good places to fish and often contain the biggest fish in the river. When looking for pools, think of a swimming hole in the river. Although sometimes smaller than that, a pool is any place where the water becomes slower and deeper than the surrounding water.

Runs connect riffles and pools. Water in a run is moving at a fairly consistent speed and

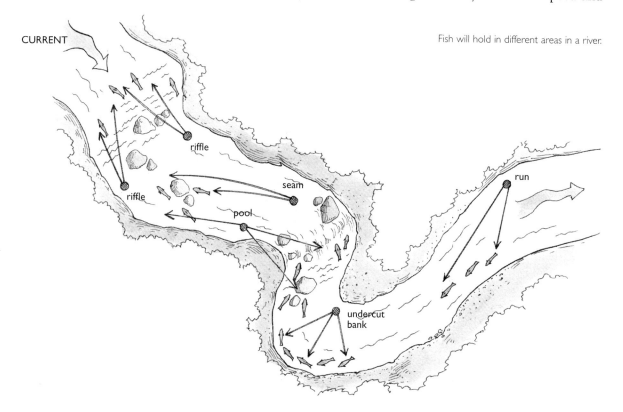

Fish will hold in different areas in a river.

depth. Think of a run as water that's wrinkly. It's not moving really fast and shallow or slow and deep. It's water somewhere in between.

Fish will be found in all these places at different times. Sometimes in the morning they will be holding in the slower water of pools. In the afternoon, as the water begins to warm up, they might move into the cooler and better oxygenated water in riffles. The very next day, you might find fish in all the runs that didn't fish well at all the day before. The fun, frustration, and intrigue of fishing is that no matter how much experience you've had, you'll never hold all the answers. I think it's the mystique and maddening problem solving that drives most anglers—that and, at times, just pure dumb luck.

Often, the satisfaction in fly-fishing comes with just figuring out where those fish are. I remember spending hours on one big river trying to find fish in different kinds of water. I had gone there on the recommendation of a friend who said the fishing was fabulous. She had been there a few days before and told me where she had been fishing and what flies had worked well. When I got to the river, it was slightly off-color and muddy from the beginning of spring runoff. I tried the flies that my friend told me were hot. No fish. I tried bigger flies, nymphs with gold beads and sparkly materials to draw attention in the murky water. No fish. Then I tried to fish a Woolly Bugger, a dark-colored streamer, hoping to swing it right in front of a fish. No fish. For hours my only bites came from the swarm of mosquitoes following me. Bug-bitten and sunburned, I thought, "there are no fish in this silly river!" Dejected, I started back to my truck.

As I was walking, I kept watching the water for fish, out of habit—and almost walked right by them! There in the quiet water just a few feet from the bank was a pack of big rainbow trout, right under the surface. They were stacked up in that water like in a fish hatchery. Trembling with excitement, I slowly backed away to watch and try to figure out what they were waiting for. And then I saw it: a large, fluttering bug the length of a toothpick and as thick as a pencil. The insect looked like a helicopter about to crash. I watched as it skimmed down to the water. Just as it touched, a large rainbow trout flashed to the front of the pack and snapped up that bug! I quickly put on the largest dry fly I had, a size #6 Stimulator, and made a short cast. Wham! Fish on! I spent the next hour catching as many of those fish as I could, squealing with glee the entire time. I learned several things that day, including the value of being a good observer, and of trying different flies in different types of water. Persistence usually, though not always, pays off with this sport.

Seams

Aside from the basic structure of riffles, pools, and runs, fish will also hold where a rock or a slight depression in the riverbed forces the river current to slow down, however slightly. As anglers, we call such an area a *seam*, a place in the water where two different speeds of current come together (see illustration opposite). Think of it as slower water meeting faster.

Some seams are easier to see than others. In water moving around a rock or log, the more obvious seam occurs downstream from the obstacle, where the structure in the water creates a slow spot. There is also a subtle seam created upstream of a place where the water is forced to push against and move around the rock.

The slowing of the current upstream of a rock is all a fish needs to take a break from its almost constant feeding, so all seams are great spots to fish. The resting spot does not have to be large; fish will hold anywhere they can get a slight break from the current. Sometimes a slight depression or back eddy is all they need to call a place home. A fish will hold in a resting spot, move out into the current to feed, and then slide back into its resting spot.

Transition zones

Fish also hold in *transition zones*, where shallow water meets deeper water, such as the edge of a shelf. These transitions can almost always be detected by color changes in the water. In rivers that are not murky or off-color, shallow water tends to be lighter in color than the deeper water. You'll find fish holding right in the line where the color changes and moving back and forth between the deeper and shallower water.

Cover

You can sometimes find fish where there is *cover* or shelter. Fish know that they must have an escape route available if they sense trouble, if a shadow or vibration in the water indicates that a predator is likely lurking nearby. Cover can come in many forms, such as overhanging brush or still shadows on the water, or riverbanks undercut by water erosion. Cover provides a place for a quick get-away if the fish sense trouble or are spooked.

Sight fishing

I've come to realize that the best way to know where the fish are holding is to see them! Sometimes I spend more time looking in the water for fish than actually fishing.

Fishing for fish you can see, or *sight fishing*, is an acquired skill. You will have a better time of it if you first locate a place that is likely to hold fish. Then look for a color or shape that is a bit out of place. Only rarely in a river do you actually see the entire fish clearly. Sometimes just a shadow or a fin or a slight movement draws your attention. Since you are looking in moving water, focus your eyes on one promising spot. You will notice that tiny windows of clarity open and close as the currents move across your target area. Keep looking: it is in these openings that you will be given a glance at an entire fish or sometimes just an object that looks fishy.

Sight fishing is a skill that will improve with time and experience. Don't feel silly if you stare at what you think is the biggest fish you've ever seen and it turns out to be only a rock. I have stalked and worked many "rock fish" in my experiences on the river. You never know—one day your rock fish might turn out to be a real fish. When in doubt, I will cast to anything suspect and then make a decision.

Reading still water: ponds and lakes

On any lake or pond, some areas are better to fish than others. Reading a pond or lake can be less complex than reading moving water because there are fewer variables. Fly-fishing in ponds or lakes can be more of a waiting game, however. Your best strategy is often just letting your fly sit in the water, twitching or moving it occasionally to draw the fish's attention. Unlike fish in rivers, which tend to be stationary and hold in certain areas, fish in a pond or lake are for the most part constantly moving. Still-water fish cannot afford to wait in one place for moving currents to bring a meal their way; they must swim around in search of food. With any luck, your fly will intersect with a moving, hungry fish.

When I go fly-fishing, I assess my mood. What kind of fishing do I feel like doing? Do I feel like doing a lot of longer casting? Do I want to cover the water quickly, or spend lots of time in one spot fishing every square inch of a run?

Inlets and outlets

Many ponds or lakes have *inlets* where freshwater flows in, bringing food for fish such as insects. Fish will sometimes stack up by the inlet of a pond, waiting for the incoming current to bring them a tasty morsel. Consequently, you fish an inlet as you would a river, casting your fly into the current and letting it drift naturally. If the pond or lake has an *outlet*, this is another good place to look. Fish will often congregate where the water is flowing out, waiting for food to drift their way.

Cover and transition zones

Fish need to feel safe in still water, just as they do in moving water. Still shadows cast on ponds and lakes provide good cover, as do weed beds or areas where you can see large underwater clumps of growth. The fish will often swim around the edge of a weed bed, looking for food and darting into or under the weeds if they sense danger from predators.

Just as in looking for transition zones in moving water, watch for any kind of change in the still water of the pond or lake. Lighter colors usually indicate shallower water. A darker color may either mean the water is deeper or indicate a weed bed. In a lake as in a river, you'll sometimes find fish right where the water changes color.

Sight fishing

Fish are easier to spot in still water than in moving water. You will sometimes see them swimming very close to the bank. When you see a moving fish, the best strategy is to cast a few feet ahead of the fish, hoping that your fly will cross the fish's path. *Rise forms*, rings made by fish taking food from the surface, are also generally easier to see on still water. If you see a rise, cast in that general area, because you know that a fish was just there.

Fishing techniques

Once you've picked a fishy-looking spot in either a lake or a river, you have to decide what method to use: dry fly, wet fly, nymph, or streamer. When I go fly-fishing, I assess my mood. What kind of fishing do I feel like doing? Do I feel like doing a lot of longer casting? Do I want to cover the water quickly, or spend lots of time in one spot fishing every square inch of a run?

There are no absolutes in fly-fishing. Someone once told me that's why we call it *fishing* versus *catching*.

How long do I fish with a fly that's not catching fish before I decide to change the fly or move on? I often wish I could carry four different rods, one rigged for each method of fly-fishing. Of course that's not practical, but there will be days when you want to do it all! And you can, too—just not all at the same time. Just think, you get to make up the rules of what you want to do and which method to choose. And you can switch to a different fly or method whenever you like.

Do you see fish rising and taking insects from the surface of the water? In this case, fishing a dry fly would be a good choice. Do you see small baitfish darting around near the banks? It might be a good time to try a streamer, which imitates a small fish. But keep in mind that just seeing small fish doesn't mean that the streamer will be "the" fly, or that you won't be able to catch a fish with a nymph or a dry fly in that same water. Don't fret over finding the "right" fly or technique. In any situation there are probably a number of different flies you can use (see chapter 9 on aquatic entomology and seining).

Fly-fishing has no hard and fast rules! One method might be more effective than others at certain times, but there are no absolutes in fly-fishing. Someone once told me that's why we call it *fishing* versus *catching*. Enjoy the whole process. I talk with many people who want to have *the* answer, but experimenting, trial and error, small or great successes are all part of the fun.

Fishing a dry fly

Fly-fishing with a dry fly such as an Adams, a Yellow Humpy, or an Elk Hair Caddis can be the most fun, because you can actually see the whole drama unfolding. You cast out a fly and watch in anticipation as it floats quietly over a fishy-looking spot. Suddenly you see a silvery flash as your fly is sucked under the water. Fish on!

Traditional or standard dry flies can be recognized by their *hackle*, the feather fibers that radiate out from the hook at a 90-degree angle to imitate the wings and legs of a flying insect. Another category of dry flies, called *parachutes*, can be identified by a white or brightly colored post sticking straight up from the fly at a 90-degree angle. Parachutes also have hackle, but their hackle radiates from the center of the post, parallel to the water's surface. Because parachute dry flies create a lower profile while floating on the water, the post is there to help the angler see it more easily. Sometimes fish prefer a traditional dry fly, which has a higher profile above the water; at other times they may favor the lower profile of the parachute dry fly. Who knows why?

I've heard anglers say that if you don't see

Left to right: Two dry-fly types, **parachute** and **traditional**.

any fish *rising*, taking insects off the top of the water, you shouldn't waste your time fishing a dry. It's true that you might be more likely to catch a fish on a dry fly when you see fish rising, but I have caught many fish on dry flies in the middle of the day without having seen one fish rise.

Suddenly you see a silvery flash as your fly is sucked under the water. Fish on!

Anglers also talk about hooking fish after fish in the midst of a heavy *hatch* when there are weather conditions such as cloud cover, rain, and even snow. (You know there's a *hatch* when you see a large number of winged insects flying or hovering just above the water; see chapter 9.) It's true that higher humidity in the air will cause newly hatched flies to linger longer on top the water, waiting for their wings to dry after hatching out of their nymphal stage. And I think that trout feel safer from predators in overcast conditions because they can't be seen as well in the water. Yet casting out a dry fly even in these situations is never a sure thing. Once when I was fishing on the Bighorn River in Montana in late April, the fish were feeding so actively at the surface that the water appeared to be boiling! I had never seen so many fish rising, and I thought to myself, "Aha! A sure thing!" But in almost an hour of changing dry flies like crazy, trying to find the right pattern, and trying to distinguish my fly from the real flies, I could not hook even one in that sea of rising fish.

Fish react differently in each situation. Some rivers are known as places where you need to be very technical in your fly selection and presentation. Anglers refer to the fish there, like those on the Bighorn, as being "selective." Everything from the size of the fly to having it drift just right in the water demands precision. But selective or "picky" fish, as I like to describe them, are generally the exception, not the rule. Most rivers have more opportunistic fish feed eagerly at each and every opportunity. They are happy to come up to grab your fly even if it isn't exactly the same size and shape. Dumb fish are fun!

The setup for a dry fly is the most basic. After you choose a fly, you simply tie it on your tippet or leader with a clinch knot (page 38). I like to use at least a 9-foot leader to fish a dry fly; the longer leader, which increases the distance between your fly and your fly line, enables a more stealthy presentation to the fish that are right under the surface. After you tie your fly on, apply some flotant to keep it dry and floating as long as possible. Although they are tied with materials that naturally repel water, dry flies will eventually become saturated and begin to sink. Flotants (see chapter 6) are silicone-based products that repel water, just like the repellent that seals your snow boots or rain jacket.

Dry-fly presentation is the most delicate kind of fly-fishing. You will have to learn to make your flies land gently on the water so as not to scare your fish. On a river, the typical approach is to work your way upstream. Fish in moving water always face toward the current, and their vision is the best and most accurate when they're viewing objects right in front of their noses. They also have good side or peripheral vision that can detect objects and movement. But every fish has its blind spot. Think about your own vision when you are driving a car or walking. You can see best

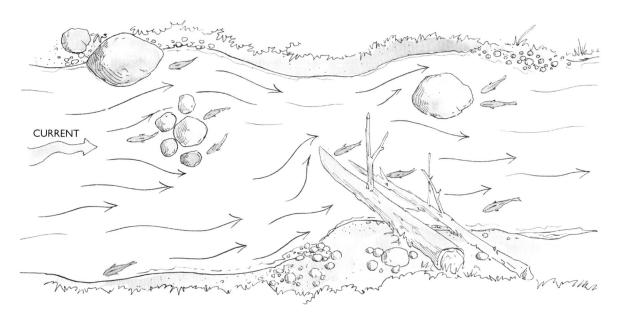

CURRENT

Fish always face the current in moving water.

directly in front of you, are aware of objects and motion to the sides, but are completely blind to what's happening behind you—unless you have a rearview mirror.

Since fish don't have a rearview mirror, working your way upstream is ideal because the fish you are stalking aren't aware of you right away. Keep a low profile if you can, and move slowly and quietly, especially if you are in the water. Don't hit your boots on rocks, splash in the water, or walk heavily on the stream bank. Fish can detect vibrations, and by the time you realize you've been too loud, they'll have darted away for cover. Scared fish don't feed; they hide.

Ideal casting in a river is called *quartering upstream.* If you stand facing a stream and hold your rod directly out in front of you, the rod makes a 90-degree angle with the bank. If you swing your arm, in the upstream direction, about halfway toward the bank at your back, you make the 45-degree angle referred to as quartering. Casting your line from this angle will enable your clear leader to pass over the fish without letting the colored fly line spook them. If you cast too far over the fish, your fly line will hit the fish on the head or pass right over the fish, doing what's called *lining the fish,* which causes them to spook. Anglers also call this *putting the fish down.*

After you make your cast upstream, your line will start drifting toward you, creating slack. You will need to strip line in, taking up the slack so your fly isn't being pulled through the water by your fly line. Taking slack in to keep your line tight as it drifts on the water will be important when a fish takes your fly and you need to set the hook. Setting the hook is done by pulling on the line, typically by raising your rod so that the tight line sets the hook into the fish's mouth. (Setting the hook and playing, landing, and releasing a fish are explained later in this chapter.)

As your fly drifts in the water, it should be moving at the same rate of speed as the current. The fish are used to seeing their surface meals moving right along with the flow, going neither slower nor faster. I like to use the analogy of a bug freeway. If all the natural insects are traveling at the same speed—say, 30 miles per hour—you want your fly to move at that same rate. If your fly is traveling at 5 miles per hour or 50 miles per hour in a 30-mile-an-hour zone, your fly will stand out and look suspicious. Sometimes, just out of curiosity or aggression, a trout will eat a fly that looks or acts differently from the naturals. But more often, the trout are looking for food that looks like all their natural food. Make your fly look and act like the natural food.

The biggest challenge to making a dry fly look natural in the water comes from what we call *drag*. Drag occurs when your fly is in one speed of current (say, close to the opposite shore of a stream) and the rest of your line is moving at a different, generally faster, speed in another (say, in the middle of a stream). Let's say you see a rock sticking out of the water 15 feet away from the bank. You think that a fish might be holding in the slow water behind it, so you cast your dry fly right there. But your fly sits there only for a brief second and then is

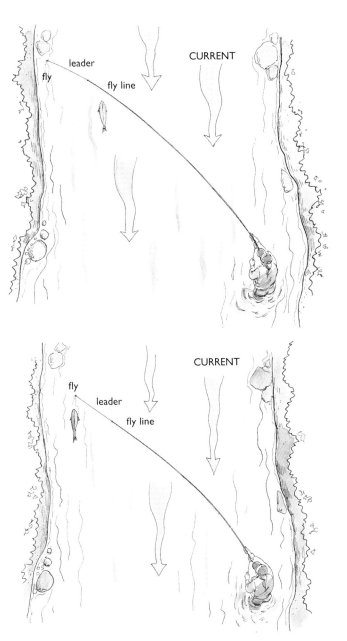

Top: An incorrect cast will **line the fish** (allow the line to pass in front of or over the fish), spooking it. **Above:** When you **quarter upstream**, your cast allows only clear leader to pass over the fish.

whipped downstream, looking as if it's skating across the water. Drag is what's yanked your fly away, and the V in the water created by the line is not a natural feature of real bugs, so fish will ignore a fly that has drag.

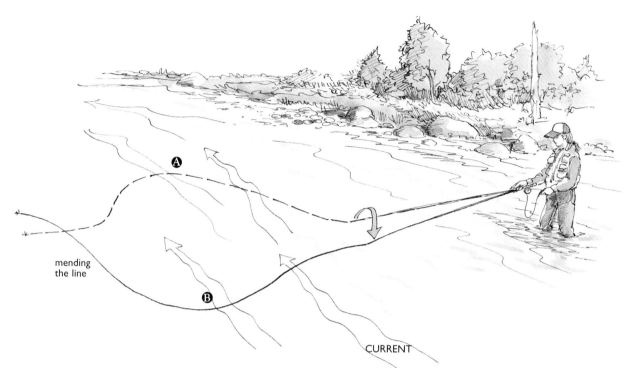

mending
the line

CURRENT

Line in position **A** creates drag. **Mending** the line in current to position **B** will prevent the fly from dragging or looking unnatural on the water.

Drag is a drag, but there is a remedy. You are going to put what's called a *mend* in the line: in this scenario, just as your dry fly lands in that slow water, flip line upstream by making a motion with your rod tip. Think of the motion you'd use to draw a half circle in the upstream direction in the air with your rod tip. Since the rod tells the line where to go, when you draw that half circle, the line will be flipped upstream. You may need to mend only once, but usually the situation requires you to make several mends, one right after the other. Mend the line only when the fly is being pulled unnaturally by the current.

Although the best approach is to walk and cast upstream, there are times when you can't. Brush or a cliff or dangerous wading situations such as drop-offs may stand in your way. In these cases, you can fish your dry fly either across the current directly in front of you or downstream.

Fishing a dry fly can be less demanding on still water than on a river because you don't have to contend with moving currents. The use of a longer, more finely tapered leader is recommended, because the fish will be able to see your fly more easily on still water than when it's being tumbled around in moving water. To fish a dry fly on a pond or lake, cast your fly out, using care not to slap the line down on the water and cause a large disturbance. After you've made your cast, tuck your fly line over the index or middle finger of your casting hand, point your rod down at the water, and begin pulling out the slack, stripping in enough line to make your fly move slightly on the water. (To review casting and line-handling techniques, see pages 57–59 on shooting line.) You want to be able to move the fly quickly at any time simply by lifting your rod up. This connection to your fly will be important when a fish *strikes* (grabs your fly in its mouth). By removing the slack in the line, you maintain a better connection to your fly, so when the fish strikes, you will be able to hook it by lifting your rod.

Fishing a nymph and wet fly

Since fish spend a majority of their time feeding below the surface of the water, using a nymph such as a Pheasant Tail, Prince Nymph, or Hare's Ear can be very productive. In a river, nymphs are meant to

Pheasant Tail **nymph** (left) and Soft Hackle Orange **wet fly** (right).

be fished below the surface, bumping right along the bottom, just above the rocks and bottom structure. In a lake or pond, nymphs can be found anywhere, from right under the surface, all the way to the bottom.

Nymphs are very compact in appearance. Flytiers often use weight such as lead wire underneath the other materials in order to make them sink. Nymphs with bead heads will sink faster than nymphs tied without beads. But regardless of whether the flies are weighted or are the bead-head style, I usually attach some sort of weight to the leader in addition, 12 to 18 inches above the nymph. In a pool, say less than about 6 feet deep, a floating fly line with weight attached to the leader will put your flies deep enough. If you are fishing a section of water more than 6 feet deep, a sinking line might be appropriate (see chapter 6).

You can use many different types of weights, such as split shot, lead-core line sections, or soft lead-type material known as *soft-weight*. The amount of weight you need will vary with each fishing situation. In deeper water or faster water you will use more weight to get your nymph down to the bottom; in shallow or slow water, you will need less or sometimes none at all.

Most weights used to be made from lead-based products. However, water wildlife were dying from lead poisoning as a result of eating fishing weights and lead shot from shotgun shells. As a result of pressure from those wanting to protect the environment and its resources, more manufacturers are coming out with weight products made from aluminum and tungsten, which are not toxic to the water or aquatic wildlife.

Wet flies and a type of fly called an *emerger*, such as the Orange Soft Hackle (also known as a Soft Hackle Orange) and the Leadwing Coachman,

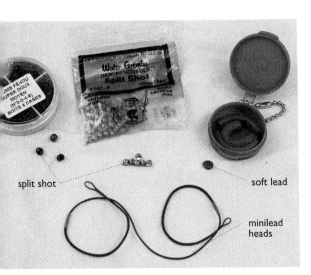

split shot

soft lead

minilead heads

When selecting **weights**, try to find products made of tungsten, aluminum, or another nonlead material.

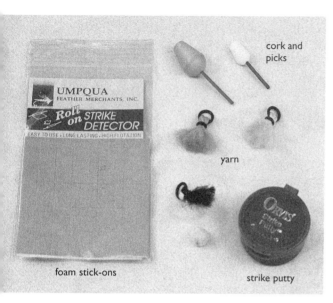

cork and picks

UMPQUA
FEATHER MERCHANTS, INC.

Roll on STRIKE DETECTOR

EASY TO USE • LONG LASTING • HIGH FLOTATION

yarn

foam stick-ons

strike putty

Strike indicators come in many forms.

are also fished below the surface. Many anglers use the term *nymphs* to include wet flies, but wet flies look different: they are tied with longer materials swept back from the eye of the hook (though they are not as long as streamers). In addition, wet flies are usually not fished as deep as nymphs.

Wet flies and emergers are intended to imitate aquatic insects that are traveling from the bottom of the water toward the surface (see chapter 9). In a river, fish will often take these wet flies as your line drifts downstream and begins to get taut from the tension of water pulling on your line. This is often referred to as having the fish "take your fly on the swing": that is, when your fly begins to swing up toward the surface. Fish may take nymphs as well when they begin to swing upward. In still water a fish will often take your nymph or wet fly as you strip line in, a motion that makes your fly appear to be moving upward in the water.

In addition to adding a weight, I recommend that you use some sort of indicator when you fish with either nymphs or wet flies. *Indicators* are brightly colored floating markers that you attach to your leader above the weight. They come in fluorescent yellows and reds and are made of foam, yarn, or putty. Since your nymph or wet fly is fished under the water surface, you will not be able to see the fish take it and you will rarely feel the strike. Instead, you'll watch the indicator for a sign that a fish is taking your fly.

For river fishing, attach the indicator at a distance above the weight to the leader approximately 1½ to 2 times the depth of the water. For instance, when fishing nymphs in a river where the water is about 2 feet deep, you place your indicator 3 to 4 feet up from your weight. In a lake, start with your indicator about 2 feet up from your fly. With this setup, your nymph will be suspended underneath your indicator, 2 feet below the surface. You might have to adjust this distance: if the fish are feeding more than 2 feet under the water, move your indicator higher up on your leader, allowing the fly to be suspended deeper.

When fishing nymphs or wet flies in a river, you want your indicator to be traveling at the same rate as the current. In some situations you will have to mend the line just as you do with a dry fly (see page 80). If your indicator slows down or stops or does anything else that is contrary to the speed of the water current, that is your sign that a fish may be taking your fly. When you see your indicator hesitate, immediately and quickly raise your rod to put tension on the line. This motion will set the hook. Remember that you are looking for a visual cue, because you will rarely feel the fish on the line.

When fly-fishing with nymphs in a river, cast or flip the line, quartering upstream (see pages 78–79) and then let your fly and line drift with the current all the way downstream until the line begins to pull or drag. You may get a strike any time your nymph is in the water, but it will usually happen while the nymph is in front of you or downstream. When fishing nymphs in a lake, cast the line out, point your rod at the water, and *strip* or pull in any slack. Once the line is straight, pull on it sharply to make your indicator *jump*—dip under the water and bob back up—and then just let it sit until the water is still again. Then strip the line again. If the indicator jumps when you are not pulling on the line, assume that a fish is eating your nymph, and raise the rod quickly to hook the fish.

> **F**ishing with nymphs has the most varied techniques of any fly-fishing method because there's no one set way to rig up your line.

Fishing with nymphs has the most varied techniques of any fly-fishing method because there's no one set way to rig up your line. You'll find regional differences, so you might want to find a local fly shop in the area where you're fishing and ask what techniques or setups are recommended there.

Fishing a streamer

Fly-fishing with a streamer, such as an Olive Woolly Bugger, or a Muddler Minnow, is exciting because you will actually feel the fish take your fly, in a river or a lake. Because you will be able to feel the strike, the fish pulling on your line, you don't need to use an indicator. Streamer fishing in a river can be productive and fun in the spring and fall when fish spawn and there are many little fingerlings in the water, which streamers imitate. It is also a method I like to use when the river water is murky and high, as it is during the spring runoff. The fish can't see as well, but they can sense and feel something moving around them in the water. Fishing with a streamer is a popular method to use in lakes as well, because there are usually a lot of minnows living in still water.

Two types of **streamers**, flies designed to move like small fish in moving water, are Muddler Minnow (left) and Woolly Bugger (right).

To fish a streamer, use a short leader about 5 to 6 feet long. (You can cut back a 7½-foot leader to the length you want.) Tie your streamer right on the end of the leader. You will also need some weight to make the streamer sink. I like to use several pieces of split-shot, ball-shaped weights that remind me of Pac-Man. The split-shot looks like a BB or a ball bearing that has a cut into which you place your leader, and then squeeze or crimp the weight with forceps (or pliers) to close the "mouth" right on the leader just above the eye of the streamer. Make sure you really clamp it tight so that it won't fling off during casting. Note that this additional weight added to your line will make your cast feel awk-

Of all the methods of fly-fishing—dry fly, nymph, wet fly, and streamer—streamer fishing is the most versatile because it's the only method you can fish in ponds, in rivers, *and* in salt water.

ward. To compensate, slow the cast down, especially remembering to pause long enough after your back cast to feel the line and weight tug backward before you begin your forward cast.

After you cast a streamer on a river, your line and fly will drift downstream with the current. As the line straightens out downstream, your streamer will look like a small fish trying to swim upstream against the current. This is where the fish will often take the streamer. By stripping in the line underneath your casting-hand finger, you can impart motion that makes the streamer look alive and teases the fish to strike. When you feel the fish pulling back on the line, raise your rod tip to get that tension on the line that hooks the fish and keeps it hooked.

If you're fishing a streamer in a pond or lake, cast out and then begin to strip the line in, making sure to stop every now and then to give the fish a chance to strike. If you are not feeling any fish strike the streamer, it probably means that you need to let the fly sink deeper in the water before you begin to strip it in. Experiment with the depth by casting the streamer out in the water and then slowly counting to five before beginning to strip it in. If you still aren't getting any strikes, try, say, seven seconds. Keep adjusting the amount of time that you let your flies sink in the water until you get a fly hooked—on the bottom or in a fish's mouth.

Of all the methods of fly-fishing—dry fly, nymph, wet fly, and streamer—streamer fishing is the most versatile because it's the only method you can fish in ponds, in rivers, *and* in salt water. In fact, the most successful saltwater technique is fishing with the streamers that imitate shrimp and small fish. The general procedure is much the same as in a big lake: when you see a fish swimming, cast the streamer ahead of it and begin to strip the fly right into the path of the fish. There are more specific techniques than I can even begin to discuss in this book, but there are magazines and general books specifically on saltwater fly-fishing, as well as books written on certain species of saltwater fish (see chapter 10).

When should you make a change?

A friend new to fly-fishing once asked me, "If the fishing is slow, how do you know when it's time to switch flies or methods, cover more water, or just call it quits?" If you ask five anglers, you are likely to get five different answers to this one. From what we know about aquatic entomology (see chapter 9), the fish are going to be eating live nymphs most of the time. After I make an educated guess about what types of nymphs are in the water, I am less likely to

There are no black and white rules, because the fish will do what it wills. Sometimes the fish will swim downstream, streaking line off your reel. Other times, it will swim right toward you!

change the fly when the fishing is slow, and more inclined to change what I'm doing with that fly, or how I'm fishing it. Sometimes a simple change like adding a little more weight will make a huge difference. If that doesn't work and I feel that I've thoroughly covered the water in that spot, I will start moving up- or downstream in search of new and different water. A wise guide once told me, "when the fishing is slow, move fast!" In other words, move on to find out where the fish are.

THE CATCH

Congratulations, you have a fish on the line—now what? I often describe playing and landing fish as the postgraduate studies program. There are no black and white rules, because the fish will do what it wills. Sometimes the fish will swim downstream, streaking line off your reel. Other times, it will swim right toward you!

Experience will be your best teacher, but there are some basic rules for what to do each time you have a fish on the line. At the first sign of a strike, regardless of what fly or technique you are using, you must get tension on the line by quickly raising your rod up and keeping it pointed at the sky. Tension on the line is what sets the hook and keeps that fish hooked.

Let the rod absorb the shock of the fight by keeping the grip pointed straight up. If the fish swims away from you, let it go by allowing

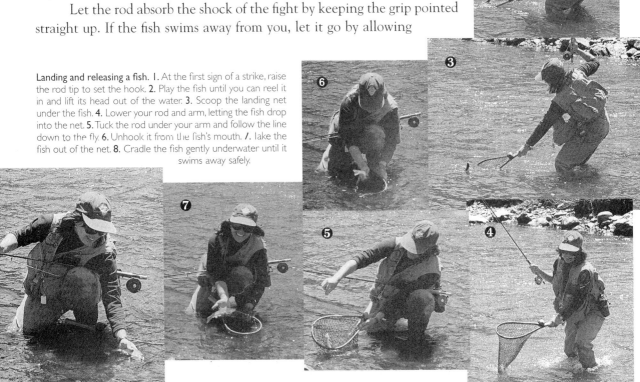

Landing and releasing a fish. 1. At the first sign of a strike, raise the rod tip to set the hook. **2.** Play the fish until you can reel it in and lift its head out of the water. **3.** Scoop the landing net under the fish. **4.** Lower your rod and arm, letting the fish drop into the net. **5.** Tuck the rod under your arm and follow the line down to the fly. **6.** Unhook it from the fish's mouth. **7.** Take the fish out of the net. **8.** Cradle the fish gently underwater until it swims away safely.

HOOK SAFETY

If you spend much time fishing, someday you will get a hook stuck in you. Most hooks have a barb on them to prevent them from slipping out of whatever they pierce. This includes waders, clothing, and body parts. Every time I go fishing, as a matter of habit and as a cardinal rule, before tying my fly on I take that barbule and press it flat with my hemostats. Then if the hook goes into something, it comes right out again, just as if it were a pin. I'm not saying that it won't hurt. It will. But at least you will be able to get the hook out more easily.

Barbed (top) and barbless (bottom) hooks.

You may be thinking that you will then also lose fish if you press the hook barbs down. Perhaps so—but once you learn how to hook a fish and play it, you will not need a barb on the hook of the fly to keep the fish on. Even if you do lose some fish, the trade-off for safety is paramount.

Make your own "barbless" hooks by pressing the hook barb flat with forceps or hemostats.

it to take out line from your reel. Only after it has made its initial run and slows down or stops will you begin reeling the line in. If the fish begins to pull again, let it take line again, and let go of the reel. I call this the *give-and-take* of playing a fish. You need tension to control the line, but if you reel or pull in line while the fish wants to run, the leader or tippet will break, and the fish will swim away with your fly stuck in its mouth.

The give-and-take process might take a while, especially if you are using a small fly on thin 5X or 6X leader. But the fish will eventually tire, and then you will be able to reel it all the way in. It's important that you get the fish in as quickly as possible so it won't be harmed by being overplayed to exhaustion, but at the same time you need to proceed with caution so you don't break the fish off the line.

When you get your fish in close to you, pull its head out of the water by raising your rod and stretching your casting arm back. When the head is out of the water, scoop your landing net underneath the fish, then lower your arm and the rod, letting the fish drop into the net.

Keep the fish in the net and the net in the water. If you are close to the bank and can easily set your rod down, do so, but make sure it is propped securely so it can't sink or float away. If you aren't close to a bank, you can tuck the rod underneath your arm while you proceed to unhook the fish.

Your hook will likely be right in the fish's lip, or on the edge of the mouth. The mouth is very hard, so the hook will not harm the fish. Larger trout have small, sharp teeth that can scrape your hand or fingers. Although the fish will not try to bite you, be careful of its teeth when you are trying to get the hook out. Grasp the fish firmly but gently in one hand (be careful not to squeeze it too hard) and with the other follow the line

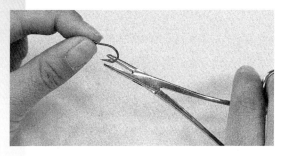

down to your fly. Back the hook out, just as if the hook were stuck in a piece of clothing. You might want to practice this beforehand on a sponge or oven mitt.

• •

I have come to realize that fish are a resource to be protected. I want to make sure that there will always be fish to catch in the water I visit.

• •

Now you must make a decision: turn the fish loose or keep it. I am a believer in catch-and-release fishing. I put back all that I catch. There was a time when I kept all my fish and fished until I caught my limit, and then the day was over. Now, I release all the fish and eat pork and beans for dinner. I have come to realize that fish are a resource to be protected. I want to make sure that there will always be fish to catch in the water I visit.

PROTECTING OUR RESOURCES

I know some fly fishers who are so adamant about catch-and-release that they would consider harming another human being before they would ever consider hurting a fish. Of course, each angler has to decide for herself, and I have certainly eaten my share of fresh trout, especially when I was camping and determined to "live off the land." But several experiences over the past few years have changed my views, and now I rarely ever keep a fish.

For example, I usually fish in fairly accessible areas, and there is one creek in particular that I love that is within twenty minutes of my home. In early spring, when the ice begins to melt and the creek begins to flow freely, I count the days until I can go out to fish that creek. As I cast my line out into the water, the fish are plentiful and healthy and hungry. I put those fish back into the creek, hoping to catch them another day. But I've noticed that as spring turns to summer, the fish become harder to find, and by late summer and fall their numbers have decreased dramatically. The few fish I do see or catch are smaller, and they are found in less likely areas of the creek. One late summer I came to the shocking conclusion that the decrease in numbers was due to the fact that people were taking the fish out of the creek. Sadly, I thought, if only they had put the fish back, there would be all kinds of fish in this creek to live to reproduce, creating even more fish.

BARBLESS HOOKS

• • • • • • • • • • • • • • •

The special hooks and flies in barbless fishing are more expensive to produce and are less widely available than standard hooks and flies.

The standard hook-making process uses the barb as a handle around which to form the hook. Creating a barbless hook requires a special step in the process to press the piece into a hook, thereby adding to the manufacturing cost.

The higher cost and general lesser availability of barbless hooks and the special flies used with them don't warrant using them, since you can make your own "barbless" flies from flies tied on barbed hooks.

HANDLING AND RELEASING FISH PROPERLY

Before releasing a fish, gently cradle it underwater so it's facing upstream.

Always be sure your hands and the landing net are wet before handling fish. The protective coat of mucus that covers their bodies is their first line of defense against bacteria in the water. Dry hands, dry nets, and nets made of stiff plastic will remove parts of this layer and leave fish susceptible to infections. Handle your fish gently, as you would handle a baby bird. Take it out of water as little as you can or, if possible, not at all.

After backing the hook out, gently cradle the fish under water with one hand under its belly and one hand holding it near the tail. Find a relatively calm place in the water where there is just a little current. The fish's nose should be facing the current. Keep your hand away from the fish's gills; they are its "lungs" and must be able to open and close freely.

As the fish begins to revive, you will see its gill plates opening and closing, and it will begin to twitch and move slowly from side to side. Stay with the fish as long as it takes. Some fish will hardly need reviving at all, and others will need you to help them for some time.

The fish will swim away from you when it's ready, but even though it is moving, do not release it in the current until it can swim vigorously. If you release a fish early and it is swept downstream by the current or turns belly up, catch it with your landing net if you can do so safely and start the process over again until the fish is able to swim away under its own power.

If the fish is bleeding profusely from the gills, or if you cannot revive it, you must do the kindest thing and dispatch it quickly. The best way I know is to take a rock or stick and hit the fish quickly and sharply on the head above its eyes. Although that sounds cruel, it is actually quick. I have never had a fish I couldn't revive, although I had one that I had to stay with for over 20 minutes.

I realize that in some areas of the country, streams are stocked, or trout are put into waters that will warm up with the heat of summer, creating an environment in which the trout can no longer survive. Those fish are expected to be caught and taken out. There are, however, many suitable creeks and streams where we should allow the trout to sur-

> If you put fish back safely, you can return to catch them again another day.

vive year-round and to reproduce year after year. Special regulations for catch-and-release fishing in certain sections of rivers and lakes has proved to increase significantly the health of a fishery, measured in the size and numbers of fish. In short, if you put all the fish back, they will live to grow larger and will spawn year after year.

Trout, unlike salmon, spawn every year of their adult lives. Depending on the water conditions and temperature, they begin anywhere between the ages of two and four and can then spawn two to four times in their average life span of six to seven years. But each trout's spawning success is precarious even in ideal conditions. Against such odds I'd like to give them as much of a chance to reproduce as I can.

While I was working in a fly shop, a man told me about a friend of his who bragged of a miraculous "wonder pool" where you could see all kinds of fish feeding and almost every other cast would put a fish on your line. One summer day this fellow convinced his friend to take him to that special secret spot. After fishing for several hours, they had hooked only two fish. His buddy couldn't believe it, because the last time he was there, he said, he had a really great day, catching over twenty fish. The other man turned to him and said, "well, I don't see even twenty fish in here now. Where'd you let 'em go, downstream?" Shocked, his friend answered, "of course not, I took them all home." It turned out that the friend had fished his glorious "wonder pool" eight or ten times, taking out six or more fish each time. It didn't take long to figure out that the wonder pool was now preserved in his freezer.

I once had an opportunity to fish a famed trout stream on the East Coast. Granted, it was early in the season, not long after opening day, but the water looked great, and the insect life was abundant and rich. Excitedly, I started fishing but was soon disappointed. I did not hook or even see a fish the entire two days I was out. I asked other anglers how they were faring, and the reports were all the same. Nothing. The locals informed me that the fish population was "nothing like it used to be in the old days." Until recent years there had been no special regulations on that river to protect and preserve its fish for future generations, and the fish had simply disappeared. Although factors such as development and water contaminants probably contributed to the dramatic decrease in the fish population, I came to the conclusion that overfishing and the absence of catch-and-release rules had to take their share of the blame. I remember thinking when I returned to my home waters that I wanted more than ever to do all I could to ensure that the fish population in the rivers and creeks I fish would remain healthy today and for generations to come.

The lesson can be learned early. I was talking with a good friend of mine who took a fly-fishing class with her ten-year-old son. They were excited to go out on their own to practice what they had learned in class, and they were both more excited when her son hooked a rainbow trout. After a glorious fight and chase, they finally got the fish into the net. It was a beautiful rainbow, although it was missing an eye, and measured over 20 inches. They took several pictures of his fish, and then the mom looked at her son and said, "well, it's time to let him go." The boy looked back at her with disbelief and bewilderment in his eyes. He wasn't ready to buy into this catch-and-release thing yet. Still, after a brief discussion he agreed. They gently revived the fish and watched it vigorously swim away. The next week, they returned to the same lucky run, and the boy caught the one-eyed fish again! He looked up at his mom and in that moment understood the concept behind catch-and-release. If you put them back safely, you can return to catch them again another day.

Chapter 6

EQUIPMENT

SELECTING A FLY ROD

One of the things that I have found to be frustrating and at times a real turnoff to a fly-fishing beginner is all the jargon. New terminology can be overwhelming, but with time and experience and simple explanations it will become more clear as it becomes more familiar. Any quality fly shop or outfitter will offer you assistance in selecting your gear and getting your outfit set up. A fly tackle dealer should answer any questions you may have and should even offer to load the line on the reel for you. But let me help you by defining some terms and explaining some available options.

No matter what type of rod you choose, make sure you try casting with it before you buy.

Most rod manufacturers offer a basic beginner package including a fly rod, reel, and line for $200 or less, though you can certainly spend more, depending on how much you want to invest in the sport. Manufacturers' top-of-the-line prices can run over $500 for the rod alone. Most rods will come with a *rod sock* and a *rod tube* or *rod case*: the sock is made from soft fabric such as heavy cotton or lightweight velour to cushion the pieces of the rod; inside the sock the rod then slides easily into a hard tube for further protection. More expensive rods offer different "actions" or flex patterns and nicer aesthetics, such as the use of nickel silver and titanium for rod components. Some makers even warrant their rods for replacement or repair no matter how the rod was broken.

No matter what type of rod you choose, you want to make sure you try casting with it before you buy. Fly-fishing shops should encourage you to cast different rods before you make a decision; ask if they'll let you take the rod outside and cast some line to test how it feels. Don't be afraid to ask for some basic casting instruction. The people who work in fly shops are usually good at educating you about the products you are considering. If you find them less than helpful, locate another shop to use as a resource. The market is too competitive for you to receive less than quality service, regardless of your skill level, ability, or gender. You may feel that you don't know enough to tell one rod from another, but believe me, you do! You don't have to be an expert to know what feels comfortable in your hand. And even if you've never held a fly rod before, with some basic helpful instruction from the shop you visit, you will most certainly like the feel of one more than another.

The last time I looked, I counted more than 90 different rods in a fly-fishing catalog. Selecting a rod can be confusing and frustrating because there is so much to choose from. When I'm helping students, we go through the same decision-making process every time.

Rod Weights

What species of fish are you mainly going to be fishing for? If you fish for silver salmon in Alaska, your rod will be different from the one you would pick for rainbow trout in the Rockies. There are different weights of rods for different fishing situations, but "weight," designated by a whole number between 1 and 14, refers not to how much the rod weighs in ounces but to the weight of the fly line that the rod is designed to cast (see also page 100 on line weights). For instance a 5-weight rod is designed to cast a 5-weight line. Rod weights 1, 2, and 3 are considered light; 4, 5, and 6 are medium; and 7, 8, and 9+ are heavy. Rods are categorized by length (feet and inches) as well as weight. An "8-foot, 4-inch, 2⅞-ounce rod for 2-weight line" can be referred to simply as an "8-foot, 4-inch 2-weight."

How many pieces?

Rods also come in two-piece or three- or four-piece types. Those of three and four pieces, sometimes referred to as *pack rods*, are convenient for backpacking or travel because they collapse into smaller packages: a 9-foot four-piece rod will break down into sections of about 30 inches in length, whereas its two-piece counterpart will break down to about 56 inches. The four-piece rods are more expensive because they have two more *ferrules*, or connections, and the trade-off for their convenience is that you have more to put together. If you compare the four-piece and two-piece versions of the same exact rod, you'll find the feel of the rods to be almost identical, so performance is not a relevant factor in your decision of which to buy. I find that my 9-foot two-piece rods will fit in most airline overhead bins. If I am traveling by plane to a fishing destination, I always carry on my rods and vest rather than have them stowed. I figure I can *fish* without a change of clothes but would be greatly disappointed if my rods and gear were lost on the way.

● ●

Recommended Rod Outfit Weights and Lengths by Fish Species

Use these recommendations as general guidelines. The best course of action is to consult a fly shop that specializes in the species of fish you're going for.

Fish Species	Weight Nos.	Lengths	Fish Species	Weight Nos.	Lengths
Freshwater			**Saltwater**		
Atlantic salmon	8–11	9'–15'	bluefish	8–10	9'–9½'
bass	6–9	8½'–10'	bonefish	7–9	9'
Pacific salmon	9–11	9'–15'	bonito	7–9	9'–9½'
panfish	1–5	7'–8'	permit	8–10	9'–9½'
pike	8–10	9'	redfish	7–9	9'
shad	7–9	9'	sailfish	12–14	9'
steelhead	7–9	9'	stripers	8–11	9'–9½'
trout	4–6	7½'–9'	tarpon	10–14	9'
			tuna	11–14	9'

Reprinted from *Orvis Fly-Fishing School Notebook*, © 1998 the Orvis Company.

● ●

Rod lengths

In addition to deciding what weight will be best for you, you'll also have to choose the length of the rod. Fly rods range in size from 6½ to 10 feet. A longer rod is easier to cast because you have more leverage to work with, but it is not ideal for all fishing situations. A small, brushy creek, for instance, may give you very little room to cast. Length selection, then, is based on where you are going to be fishing most of the time. If you think you'll do most of your fishing in larger rivers and lakes, a 9-foot rod would be a good choice. If you want to fish some of those brush-lined creeks with a lot of trees at your back and very few open spaces, perhaps a 7½- to 8-foot rod would be right for you. Ten-foot rods are designed for anglers fishing from a float tube (see chapter 8) because the additional length helps to keep the line off the water when it's being cast. I also know a friend who likes a 10-foot rod when he fishes from a canoe because the extra length allows him to reach his rod around the prow.

If you start a rod collection, be sure to select rods different enough to use in different situations and perhaps for different species of fish. Don't fill your closet with 5- and 6-weight rods of 8½ to 9 feet in length, because these rods, though slightly different, can all be used in the same place for the same types of fish. I have a 9-foot, 5-weight rod for all my trout fishing on larger rivers. I also have a 6-foot, 6-inch, 2-weight rod for fishing small creeks where the fish are mainly 6- to 8-inch trout. The 2-weight rod is fun to use, but I save it for small, tight areas because it's considerably more difficult to cast.

Rods for women

When a popular fly-fishing magazine published an article entitled "Should Women Have Their Own Fly Rods?" I just about ripped the magazine out of my friend's hands, outraged at the impli-

● ●

If you start a rod collection,
be sure to select rods different
enough to use in different
situations and perhaps for
different species of fish.

● ●

cation that a woman need not own her rod but could just borrow any old rod from a friend. Actually, the article was about fly rods designed for use mainly by women. Although there is ongoing controversy among fly tackle dealers, manufacturers, and women guides and anglers about the need for specialty women's rods, most major rod companies do carry a line of rods for women. They are generally 8 to 9 feet in length, range from 4 to 8 weights, and are lighter in ounces than their unisex counterparts. The main feature differentiating them from other rods, however, is their slimmer grip. Women generally have smaller hands than men, so we can more comfortably wrap our hand around a smaller grip.

Grips come in different shapes (see photo on page 27). The most common grip on a medium-weight rod is a *reversed half wells*. Grips on women's rods also include modified *cigars*, and even one with a thumb depression sanded into the handle which makes it fit nicely in the hand. It's important that you find a rod with a grip that feels comfortable in your hand and not as if you are holding a paper towel tube. Your hand will become fatigued more quickly if you try to hold onto a large, cumbersome grip all day. My advice to you is to try several rods, both the specialty rods for women and the unisex rods. The feel of a rod is purely subjective; the key is your comfort.

Different flexes

Another factor in your selection has to do with rod *flex*. Fly rods are made of various materials, including graphite and fiberglass. Traditionally, they were made from bamboo. Bamboo fly rods are still available today; they are aesthetically beautiful and should be regarded as treasured art objects, but they are seldom practical for the beginner because they are heavy and expensive. Since each rod is handmade from planed bamboo and composed of six different individual pieces, a bamboo rod at $1,000 is considered a deal; prices upward of $3,000 are more commonplace. In addition, the action or flex of bamboo is the slowest of all materials, meaning that the rod moves the line very slowly, taking its time to bend and unbend in order to load.

In the 1970s rod manufacturers began producing rods of fiberglass, trying to imitate the slow action or movement of bamboo at an affordable price. But fiberglass is almost too soft, feeling something like a limp noodle and providing little or no control or power in the cast.

Graphite, which came on the scene in the late 1970s, is now the most commonly used material. Graphite rods are an excellent choice because the graphite is extremely lightweight for its strength. Keep in mind that since at times you will have to make 25 to 50 casts for one fish, you'll want a rod that is light in your hand and isn't a bulky burden.

Graphite rods have different flexes. Some are called *full-flex*, *slow-action* or *soft* rods (terms that are used interchangeably), meaning that the rod bends easily through its entire length. A slow-action rod takes longer to load, or bend, so the line will take longer to straighten out in your back

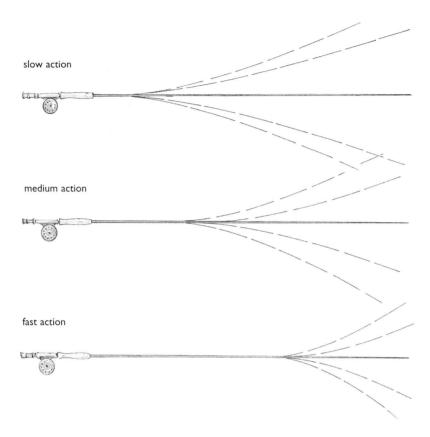

slow action

medium action

fast action

Different **flexes** or **actions** of fly rods.

cast. For casting purposes, this means a longer pause is needed in your timing. A *medium-flex* or *medium-action* rod has its flex point toward its midsection. A *tip flex* rod, also called a *fast-action* or *stiff* rod, feels very stiff throughout its length and has most of its bend in the tip. Both medium- and fast-action rods will load or bend more quickly, causing the line to shoot into your back cast more quickly, so you need a shorter pause.

How do you know which flex to choose? A fly tackle dealer can help you decide about length and weight on the basis of where you'll be spending most of your fishing time, but let the deciding factor be what flex feels good. When you cast the different rods, you'll know what works best for you. Some rods that you cast and handle will feel bulky and awkward. Others will fit in your hand well and just feel right when you cast. Take your time when you're selecting a rod, because with any luck you will have it for a long time.

I recommend that you consider investing the extra dollars needed to purchase a rod with at least a twenty-five year guarantee against breakage or damage for any reason. The difference in price will be around $100, but I believe you'll find it worth the investment in the long run. No matter how careful you are with your gear, car doors and boats love to eat rods. If you break a rod that

GETTING DIRT OR SAND OUT OF THE REEL

. . . .

Take care never to set your reel down on gravel or dirt or sand, which will get inside the reel, most likely between the spool and the frame. If you do get grit in your reel and the spool is rubbing against the frame, just remove the spool and dip both the frame and the spool with its line in the water to wash the grit away. Otherwise, it will grind against the gears in the reel causing the spool to lock up and the mechanism to wear out. When fishing in salt water, take special care to rinse the corrosive salt off your rod and especially your reel and line after every use.

does not have a guarantee, though, you can always send it back to the manufacturer for repair. Most manufacturers then provide an estimate of the cost. To give you an idea, a new tip for a rod may run $80 to $100. Always send back all the sections of the rod together, even if only one is broken. Making a replacement requires sizing the pieces together by hand, and the manufacturer should have all parts to ensure they will fit back together.

You may have seen rods that are a spinning and fly-fishing combo, but I suggest that if you both spin and fly fish, you should have a separate rod for each. Your cast is the basis of fly-fishing, so give yourself the best advantage you can to make casting easier with a rod designed specifically for casting a fly line.

SELECTING A REEL

When I was learning about fly-fishing gear, understanding the reel didn't seem important; I thought the reel was just a place to store the line. In the beginning, this is true. It wasn't until I began to catch fish consistently, and then larger fish, that I learned what made an expensive reel different from a basic one.

A reel has a frame and a spool. The frame holds and controls the spool, and the spool actually holds the line. A reel usually comes with a padded case to protect it during storage. Reels range in cost from $29 to over $400. The main differences are in their construction, use of materials and features. More affordable reels have some plastic parts, and their metal parts are manufactured separately and then fitted together. More expensive reels are machined or shaved from solid, lighter, stronger metal.

Spools

On most reels there is a spring-loaded latch that you can press to release the spool from the frame. You can have several spools to use with one frame: for instance, one spool with a floating line for most types of fishing and another with a sinking line to use in lakes or in the deep pools or runs of a river. Spools cost usually about half the price of the whole reel. For instance, a spool for a $100 reel may cost around $50.

If you have rods of different weights, such as a 5-weight and a 6-weight rod, you can use the same reel for both and simply have one spool with a 5-weight line and another spool with a 6-weight line. Since the 5-weight line is thinner and will take up less room on the spool than the 6-weight line, it's best to put more backing under it to fill up the reel. Most reels come with a chart that details the recommended size of line and how much backing the reel will hold in addition.

When you purchase a reel, consider investing in an additional spool. You will not only have the option of using the same reel for different lines but also have a spare in case you damage a spool. Because manufacturers often discontinue certain models as newer reels are introduced each year, finding a replacement spool can be a challenge.

Reel Size

Reels come in different sizes to balance

When you purchase a reel, consider investing in an additional spool. You'll not only have the option of using the same reel for different lines but also have a spare in case you damage a spool.

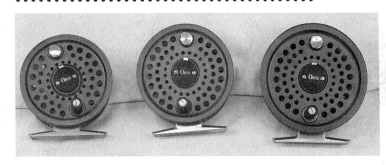

The larger the spool diameter of the reel, the higher the corresponding line weight number.

the different weights of rods. Smaller reels with a small spool diameter such as 2¾ inches are designed for use with rod weights of 1, 2, and 3. The fly lines that are cast with those lighter-weight rods are thinner and therefore take up less room on a reel. There are medium-sized reels with a spool diameter of, say, 3¼ inches for rod weights 4, 5, and 6, and larger reels, with diameters of perhaps 3¾ inches for rods of 8, 9, or 10 weight. The thicker lines used for heavier-weight

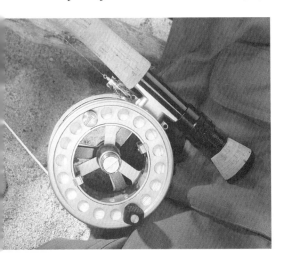

Large-arbor reels have a larger diameter core so that each revolution of the reel winds a greater length of line.

rods take up more room on a reel. One style of reel is usually offered in different sizes, all with the same features and design, the only difference being the diameter of the spool.

From our discussion of backing (see pages 64–65) you know that one end of it is attached to the arbor, or core, of the reel and the other end the fly line. The backing serves to fill up the reel, allowing the line to be wrapped in larger coils. There are *large-arbor reels* that have a thicker core around which the backing and fly line are wrapped. With a large-arbor reel the fly line is wound in very large coils or loops, allowing the angler to retrieve greater amounts of line with each revolution of the spool, or turn of the handle.

Drag systems

All reels have a drag system that provides the resistance or tension when line is being either reeled in or pulled off the reel. Without a drag system, the spool would "free spool," meaning that if you gave the line a quick, sharp pull, it would just keep coming off the reel and end up in a tangled mess. There are two basic types of drag systems for reels, plus many different features and characteristics from which you can choose.

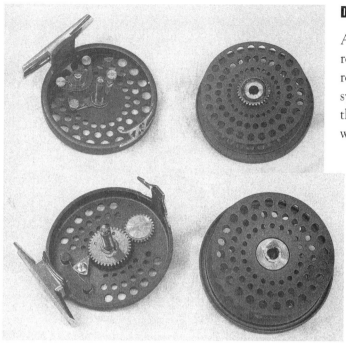

Top: **Spring-and-pawl drag reels** have a small range between the lightest and the heaviest drag setting. **Above:** On **disc drag reels**, there is a significantly greater difference between the heaviest and the lightest drag setting.

Spring-and-pawl reels

In a *spring-and-pawl drag* system, a spring pushes against a *pawl* (a triangle-shaped piece of metal or plastic), which presses against a gear in the middle of the spool, creating tension. Most spring-and-pawl reels have a knob that you can tighten or loosen to create more or less resistance when the line is being pulled off the spool. The amount of tension you use is determined by the strength of the leader you are using. For lighter, thinner leaders and tippets, such as 5X or 6X, you will want to use the lightest drag setting so that a fish can take line off of the reel without causing the leader material to break. For heavier, thicker leaders and tippets of 3X or 4X, you can adjust your reel to a heavier drag setting, using the resistance to slow down the fish.

In spring-and-pawl drag systems there is little difference between the lightest and the heaviest setting. I have a very delicate spring-and-pawl reel that I use with fine leaders and tippets, because the reel's lightest drag setting allows the fish's slightest movements to take line off my reel instead of breaking the leader. A spring-and-pawl reel is also adequate for fish under 12 inches because they generally don't pull very hard, and you can also simply strip the line in with your line hand to land them.

Disc drag systems

A *disc drag* system works on the same principle as the spring-and-pawl: it's designed to control the tension on the line and has a knob that you use to adjust for more or less resistance. But the disc drag has an added gear, attached to the frame of the reel, that dramatically increases the amount of tension you can have while the fish is trying to take line off of the reel. Disc drag reels are heavier than spring-and-pawl reels and there is a lot of difference between the lightest and the heaviest setting.

FLY LINES

Purchasing a fly line can be a mystery. You will be asked, what taper? what weight? floating or sinking? It can be confusing! Let me go through each variable so you will be informed and prepared before you set out to buy one. Fly lines can cost anywhere from $25 to

When casting, you're actually casting the weight of the fly line, not the weight of the fly.

$60, depending on the type, the length, and any special features such as coatings that make them easier to cast.

The life of a fly line will depend on how often you use it and how you take care of it. It will last much longer if it is cleaned regularly with line cleaner or a mild soap after several uses, although each line is different, and it's best to follow the manufacturer's instructions for line care. You'll notice that most wear occurs at the end of your line to which you attach your leader, especially the front 15 feet. It's time to replace the fly line when it starts to develop hairline cracks in the coating, when it becomes discolored or stained with dirt that won't clean off, or when pieces of the coating begin to peel away. In areas of high humidity, you always want to dry your line completely before storing it for any length of time, or else it will likely stick to itself.

Taper

When casting, you're actually casting the weight of the fly line, not the weight of the fly. The fly line does not, as I once assumed, remain the same diameter throughout its length but tapers in thickness. Fly lines are available in different tapers.

Weight forward

In a weight-forward line, the end where you'll attach your leader may have the diameter of, say, vermicelli pasta. About 8 feet into the line, it thickens to about the diameter of spaghetti. It remains spaghetti thickness for about 35 feet, then returns to the vermicelli thickness again, here called *running line*. This taper allows the line to be cast with the heavy, thick part called the *belly* flicked forward and the thinner running line trailing after it. For most beginners, I advise the use of a weight-forward line, as it is the most common and easiest to handle when you are learning to cast.

to leader ◄······   belly   running line   ······► to backing

to leader ◄······   belly   ······► to backing

Profiles of **weight-forward** (top) and **double-taper** (bottom) fly lines.

Double taper

A double-taper line actually has two fishable tapers. The end to which you attach your leader, as in the weight forward line, starts out thin and then gets thicker. Instead of tapering back down to a thin running line, however, it remains thick for most of its length before tapering down again toward the end that is attached to the backing. The advantage of the double taper is that when the forward part of the line gets badly worn, you can take all the line off the reel, cut it from the backing, and reverse it, tying the worn end to the backing, and having a "new," hardly used section of fly line to fish with. (For the Albright knot, used to tie fly line to backing, see page 65.) The disadvantage is that double-taper line will not cast for distance (over 35 feet) as well as a weight-forward line.

Weight

As with fly rods (see page 92), when fly fishers refer to the "weight" of their line, they use a whole number between 1 and 14. This number designates not the weight of the rod and fly line in physical ounces (although there's a correlation) but the type of rod and line. The weight of the rod should be balanced with the weight of the line you are using, meaning a 5-weight rod should be used with a 5-weight line. The weight you use has to do with where you fish and what you are going to be fishing for.

Floating versus sinking

Another variable in fly lines is whether they are made to sink or float. A code is used to designate a line that floats (F), sinks (S), or is a sink-tip line (F/S or S/T) with a tip that sinks while the rest floats. In deciding which one to buy, decide first where you are going to fish. Floating lines

Fly lines come in different colors and weights. Here, weight-forward pale yellow 8-weight line (left) and double-taper gray 2-weight line (right).

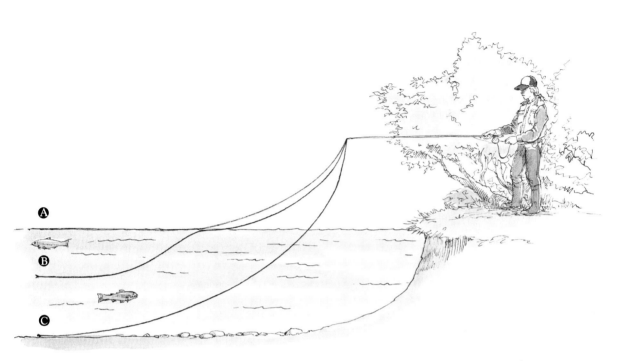

Floating fly line (**A**), sink-tip fly line (**B**), and sinking line (**C**).

are used 90 percent of the time on rivers and lakes where fish are feeding not more than 5 to 8 feet below the surface.

Sinking lines and sink-tip lines are better where the fish are feeding deeper underwater than a weighted leader on your floating line can normally reach. They are useful on a pond or lake or a really deep pool in a river. I carry one reel and two spools loaded with two different lines, a floating and a sink-tip line in order to be prepared for any situation I may encounter on the water. Sinking lines come in different "classes," based on how fast they sink. For example a class 4 line sinks at a faster rate than a class 2 line.

Color

Fly lines come in many different colors, and the color you choose is for the most part personal preference. All sinking lines are dark—dark green or dark brown—so that they are less easily seen by the fish in the water. A dark color is fine for you, too, since you aren't trying to see a line that's underwater.

Some anglers also prefer gray or dark brown floating lines for a more stealthy presentation. When you're first starting out, however, I recommend a light line that can be easily seen, perhaps pale yellow or green. Being able to see your line on the water will help you to find your fly.

> **W**hat you wear will depend entirely on where you are going fishing and when.

DRESS FOR SUCCESS

One of my mom's favorite questions when we are going anywhere is "What are you wearing?" I get the same question from students who are going fishing for the first time. What you wear will depend entirely on where you are going fishing and when. You probably know whether you are a warm person or a cold person. Some people can be freezing when it's 75°F in the sun. Others can be comfortable wearing only a T-shirt when it's below freezing. Pick and choose your clothing accordingly. In most cases, you'll probably be wearing a pair of waders (described later in this chapter), to keep you dry as you step or stand in water.

Clothing color

Choose clothing in colors that blend well into your surroundings. I usually dress in environmentally friendly greens, blues, tans, and other dark colors when I'm fishing in the mountains. Fish have color vision and may be spooked if they detect a bright color overhead. I've been in situations when color didn't seem to make a difference, but at other times my white T-shirt was enough to scare fish away before I could make even one cast. To be on the safe side, I recommend wearing earth tones when fishing trout streams and lakes. In salt water you probably want to wear lighter colors that blend with the water and sand. Lighter colors will also help you to keep cool when the sun is beating down.

Layering

If you fish in the mountains, you will get used to being prepared for weather that can range from hot to cold and rainy in one day. Because of these quick and sometimes drastic weather changes, I've learned to pack and wear clothing that works in layers. Everything I wear for fishing, both on my upper body and underneath my waders, is made from materials that wick away moisture, usually perspiration, allowing them to dry quickly and prevent me from getting chilled. Quick-drying materials will also dry out more quickly if you get seriously wet. The only natural fabric that fits this bill is wool, but there are various synthetics to choose from: fleece, polypropylene, Capilene, and Thermax, to name a few. Garments made of these are available at outdoor supply stores and also at some fly-fishing shops.

Wherever you go fishing, you should always take an extra full set of clothing to change into, all the way down to your underlayers. Hypothermia, a condition caused by having your core temperature cool, can set in quickly if you are wearing wet clothes. The air temperature does not have to be below freezing; hypothermia can happen even when the temperature is in the 50s or 60s.

> **A**lways take an extra full set of clothing to change into, all the way down to your underlayers.

Under your waders

No matter what season I fish, unless it is blistering hot, I always wear long underwear or tights under my waders. In early spring or fall I choose heavy thermal underwear that keeps me warm. I wear a pair of lightweight shell pants made of Supplex over my long underwear so I don't feel "naked" while I'm getting into my waders. In very cold conditions I simply put more layers on top of my thermals, such as fleece pants or another pair of leggings.

On warmer days I wear a pair of running or workout tights or just my lightweight shell pants. Wearing jeans under waders is uncomfortable because jeans are bulky and tend to bunch up and restrict movement. Sweatpants or comfortable cotton pants will do but are not ideal because they retain moisture. In hot weather you can wear shorts comfortably if you have breathable waders (described on pages 105–6); otherwise, your legs will get wet and clammy from perspiration.

Use a layering method for your upper body as well. Next to my skin I wear breathable lightweight materials such as Capilene. If it's cold out, I add a fleece top or a wool sweater, both very warm for their weight. On top of that, I wear a shell, either a wind shirt or a windbreaker, to keep my body heat in and the wind out. A windblocking layer is light in weight and can be worn over just a T-shirt or on top of heavier layers. You'll be pleasantly surprised at how warm you'll be when a

A **wind shirt** (right) is lighter weight than a windbreaker. A **rain jacket** (below) can substitute for a wind shirt or windbreaker.

FISHING GEAR FOR WOMEN
• •

Until a few years ago there was not much fishing gear made for women, and you would have to make do with the closest-fitting men's size. Trying to fit into men's waders usually meant that the body of the garment would be too long, rubbing up underneath your armpits, and the feet too big—hardly comfortable for fishing all day. Today, most of the fly tackle manufacturers are catering to women, who are rapidly entering the sport. The first women's waders and vests were designed to be more frill and fashion than function, and there are still companies who design women's products with less durability than men's. Perhaps they think that we will not fish as often or as hard as men. In fact, though some women limit the use of their equipment to a few trips a year, there are men who won't fish as much as some women will. I believe everyone should invest in quality gear that will last a long time, whether you fish 100 days a year or once every other year.

Women's waders and vests are generally smaller and cut to fit a woman's shape. The waders usually have more material in the legs and hip area, the inseams tend to be shorter, and the feet are proportionally smaller than men's. The vests are also cut shorter and some have detailing such as an elastic band on the bottom or stays on the sides to make them fit more stylishly.

At first I was thrilled at the prospect of having manufacturers market a line of women's products. Over the last few years, however, I've realized that people have individual shapes and sizes. I have worked with both men and women who were either too small or too large to fit standard sizes, so I've come to the conclusion that you should just pick the best fit, especially since manufacturers use different sizing. That may mean trying on both women's and men's waders, boots, and vests, basing your choices on comfort, fit, and the features and style you like best. If you still have a problem, try one of the companies that custom-fit waders and boots.

Don't settle for a piece of gear that doesn't fit well from the start. No matter how good a bargain you think you're getting, things that don't fit, especially waders, will cause you frustration and discomfort every time you put them on, and you will probably be less likely to fish and enjoy yourself out there.

windbreaker keeps that wind from whisking away your body heat. Some manufacturers have combined fleece with a wind shell, perfect for those chilly mornings and evenings when the sun is low on the horizon.

Make sure you have a rain jacket with a good hood, which you can also use as a windbreaker even if it's not raining. I carry my rain jacket tucked in the back pocket of my vest, often looking like a hunchback, but when you need your jacket, you don't want it to be a half-mile away. Get one large enough to wear over your vest and on the outside of your waders. A rain jacket worn under your vest will allow the contents of the vest to get saturated quickly in a downpour, and they'll often take hours to dry out. And tucking your rain jacket inside your waders will allow the water to pour inside; it's something that you'll probably do only once.

Hands and feet

No matter what the temperature is, I always wear wool socks with liners inside my waders. Light liners under wool socks keep me from getting blisters and provide insulation while keeping my feet dry. If your feet get cold easily, consider wearing several pairs of socks. Layering for your feet will provide air pockets of warmth. Calf-length socks provide more warmth and serve as well to protect your lower legs from any rubbing inside your waders. For really cold weather you might want to put small chemical heat packs inside your socks to keep your feet warm.

Gloves are a pleasure to have any time of the year when the sun dips below the horizon. I always carry a pair in my vest. Your hands will get cold, especially if they're wet from handling a fish, and if you are bundled up, you may not have pockets accessible to warm your hands. Fingerless gloves are great because they keep the majority of your hand warm while allowing you the dexterity you need for tying knots and handling your line. Some fingerless gloves come with a mitten top that you can flip back when you need to use your fingers and then flip over your fingers again to keep them warm. Don't get gloves that fit tight or even just right; instead, choose a pair at least one size larger so that the warm air can circulate around your hands. Tight gloves will make your hands colder than none at all. When you get a fish on the line, take your gloves off and tuck them in your waders or in a pocket before you put your hands in the water, then wipe your hands dry before returning them to your dry gloves. Once gloves get wet on a cold day, they rarely dry out again.

Hats

I feel naked if I'm fishing without a hat. A brimmed hat keeps the sun off your face, allows you to see into the water more clearly, and keeps the hair out of your eyes on windy days. I've heard that you can lose 80 percent of your body heat through the top of your head. I know a hat keeps me warmer, especially on cold or windy days. I prefer one with a neck cord so that if the wind blows the hat off my head, it won't go downstream. If I wear a baseball cap, I clip a hat "leash" onto both my cap and my shirt.

WADERS

If you have seen people fly-fishing, you probably noticed their waders. Waders are either hip boots or chest-high, one-piece suits waterproofed to keep you dry as you walk around in the water. You will often need to step in the water or in wet and muddy areas to fish or to get to different fishing places, and remaining dry often equates with keeping warmer. But the choice to wear waders or not has to do with your environment. Where are you fishing? In balmy ocean water you can probably just wear a pair of shorts. On a dock or in a boat, you won't need waders unless you plan to step into the water.

You can also certainly fish in most places without wearing waders. In fact, when I was first starting out, I never wore them. I would just put on a pair of old sneakers that I called my "river

> **T**he choice to wear waders
> or not has to do with your
> environment.

shoes" and, wearing shorts, step right into the water and start fishing. My dad was amazed that I could spend hours happily fishing in icy cold streams as my legs turned bright red. He came to know that after I lived through the initial shock of 45°F water running around my legs, I became numb to the cold and was so focused on fishing that I didn't care! I would have towels to dry off after fishing and dry clothing to change into at the end of the day. For consecutive days of fishing, though, especially when I was camping, I would have to worry about drying out socks and wading shorts for the next day, or face the chilly prospect of putting on wet clothing.

It wasn't until after I had my first pair of waders that I knew what I had been missing. I no longer had to thaw my legs out after fishing or worry about my shorts getting wet. Even so, when I fish small streams in nice warm weather, I still sometimes leave my waders behind, put on lightweight wading shoes and shorts, and enjoy the freedom of wading without waders, which is referred to as *wet wading*. (If you are going to wet-wade, I recommend that instead of sneakers you wear boots that have felt on the soles, described in the next section.)

My first pair of waders were awful! They were brown and made of rubber that punctured easily if I sat on a rock or got a stone inside my boot. The good thing is that they were so affordable they were almost disposable. If those rubber waders began to leak or had a tear, I would just toss them out and buy another pair. But they were hot and made me smell like a rubber balloon on a hot day (great for weight loss, because I would sweat out a good five pounds of water in a full day of fishing). Thank goodness wader technology has come a long way since then!

Chest waders versus hippers

Waders come in different lengths. There are *chest waders*, *waist waders*, and hip boots, often called *hippers*. A common notion is that women probably aren't going to wade into chest-high water, so

we should get waist waders or hip boots. I rarely see anyone, man or woman, wading out into chest-high water, nor would I recommend it from a safety standpoint. So why have chest waders? Keep in mind that the purpose of having waders is to remain dry. If you stumble and fall, or if you kneel or crouch in the water, waist waders and hip boots are going to be more likely to fill up with water than chest highs. I do have a pair of hip boots because they are convenient and easy to use. But I wear them only when I fish very small streams on hot days so that if I do stumble and fall into the water, the worst thing that happens is that I get

Wear a **wading belt** over waders to make yourself more buoyant.

wet. I never use hippers in larger rivers or streams because of the possibility of their filling up with water, which makes getting out of the water a dangerous challenge. Most of the time I'm wearing chest waders, which can also be rolled down and clipped or belted around the waist.

A *wading belt*, which is made from elastic or webbing, should always be worn with chest waders. If you fall in the water, a snug wading belt will not keep the water out of your waders completely but will slow it down considerably. The belt helps to trap air around your legs, creating an air pocket that keeps you more buoyant and gives you time to find safety (see chapter 7).

Bootfoot versus stockingfoot

Another factor to consider is whether you want *bootfoot* or *stockingfoot waders*. Bootfoot waders come with the boot permanently attached. They are convenient because they are one piece. You don't have to worry about forgetting your boots or losing one boot. In freezing conditions they have no laces to freeze up, and they tend to keep you considerably warmer because you get greater air circulation.

They have several drawbacks, however. You'll find that bootfoots are significantly heavier than stockingfoots and more cumbersome to pack or carry. And because the built-in boots are reminiscent of flimsy rubber rain boots, they do not provide the good ankle support you need when you're walking on slippery, bowling-ball-shaped rocks in the water. (Even walking alongside the river, I have jammed my foot between rocks and been thankful to have a sturdy boot to protect my ankle.) Also you don't have the option of using the boots separately if you just want to wet-wade in shorts, without the waders. If you do purchase bootfoot waders, check to make sure the connection between the wader leg and the attached boot is smooth. If the connection is rough, wear a calf-high sock to protect your shin and calf from being rubbed raw.

Stockingfoot waders, which will remind you of the "footy pajamas" you had as a child, are worn with a separate

Chest-high waders (1) and hippers (2). Bootfoot waders (3) have the boot permanently attached, whereas stockingfoot waders (4) must be worn with a pair of wading boots.

Gravel guards prevent rocks from getting lodged between your wader and boot.

PATCHING YOUR WADERS

• • • • • • • • • • • • • • • •

If your waders start to leak, most can be patched, unless they are completely ripped apart. Use a product such as Aquaseal, designed specifically for wader repair, which can be used on rubber, nylon, and breathable material. Locate the general area that is leaking and then closely examine every inch until you find a suspicious spot. It's likely that you will see a small tear or puncture. For a good patch, treat both sides of the leak, one side at a time. Place a piece of tape on one side of the damaged area, and liberally coat the other side with the repair material. Most products will take a few hours to dry completely. When this side is set, coat the other side and let it get thoroughly dry before using the waders. If you tear your breathable waders, use a needle and thread to stitch the edges together and before treating this new seam with Aquaseal or a similar product.

pair of boots designed to be submerged in water. They are not as convenient or quick to get into, because you have to put on the waders and then put on boots over them. You'll find, however, that you'll get a better fit and more support with a separate boot.

With stockingfoot waders, you should also have a pair of *gravel guards* to seal off the seam between your waders and boots. Gravel guards prevent rocks and sand from getting into your boots, which is not only uncomfortable but causes wear on the bottoms and heels of your waders. Some waders come with a set of gravel guards. I prefer the ones made of a band of elastic Velcro fastener that wraps around the top of the boot. These are easier to put on and keep out more debris than other types.

Selecting wader material

There are affordable waders made of rubber or plastic that cost around $30, but they are not the most comfortable or durable. Another choice is neoprene, a spongy foam material that is reminiscent of a skin-diving suit. When wearing neoprene waders you are completely sealed inside, so the water is kept away from your skin. Neoprene also allows you to move freely because it's stretchy, unlike rubber or plastic, and it comes in thicknesses ranging from 2 to 5 mm. The most common and versatile thickness is 3 mm, which keeps you relatively warm and insulated from the cold and is not overly hot in warmer weather. Neoprene waders range in cost from about $60 to $200, depending on the thickness and features such as pockets or reinforced knee and seat areas.

Rubber, plastic, and neoprene waders all prevent water from coming in, but these materials unfortunately are not water-permeable, so any moisture that gets inside stays inside. In really hot weather you'll become wet inside your waders from your own perspiration. In colder conditions, if you move around a lot, your perspiration will make you feel damp and clammy.

Several years ago wader manufacturers started to market what they refer to as "breathable technology," waders made from a material that prevents water from coming in but allows perspiration to be wicked away from the skin and out through the breathable membrane. They are relatively thin and light in weight. Different manufacturers combine breathable technology with different fabrics on the outside. Some outer fabrics feel very thin, and much like a shell-type windbreaker.

> **I** virtually live in my breathable waders and wear them whenever I go fishing, no matter the season.

Other breathable waders have a thicker outer fabric that is likely to be more abrasion resistant.

Worn alone, these waders provide absolutely no insulation from the cold water, which is a great benefit in warm weather. In colder conditions you can put on as many layers under them as you need, as I found out in Montana in the middle of a wet snowstorm. Though wearing just about every piece of clothing I owned under my neoprene waders, I soon got chilled and felt extremely cold and clammy. Yet my friends said that they were toasty warm and dry. They were all wearing breathable waders with proper layering underneath. My first purchase when I got home was a pair of breathable waders, which I have virtually lived in since and wear any time of the year I go fishing.

Breathable waders range in cost from around $130 to $300, depending on their features and outer fabric. They are a pleasure to wear because they are lightweight and very comfortable. You'll feel as if you're fishing in your favorite sweatpants. The drawback is that they are not as tough on the outside as the neoprenes and will not take the abuse of sliding against rocks and brush as well.

General features and fit

Whatever material or style you choose, there are some general features that you want to keep in mind. If you have the choice, purchase waders that come with reinforced knees and seat. These are the two areas that get the most wear.

The waders should fit comfortably but not be tight. You will need to layer clothing underneath when it's cold and still have enough room to be able to "high step" over rocks or logs. If you are trying on stockingfoot waders, make sure the feet are not skin tight, because a tight fit will make your feet cold. Wear your fishing socks when you try on waders; heavy wool socks will take up more space.

Look for shoulder straps made of elastic rather than rough webbing; elastic is more comfortable to wear all day.

Wading Boots

If you select stockingfoot waders, you'll need a pair of wading boots, which range from $30 to $125. They are designed to be submerged in water, so they should be made of material that won't deteriorate or shrink in repeated use. The two main features to consider are fit and protection. Wading boots are meant to be oversized, since you wear them over your waders. Most come only in whole sizes, and if you have to choose between a bit tight and a bit loose, go with the larger pair. Wading boots are not supposed to fit as close as a hiking boot, and the extra room will allow for good circulation in your feet, helping to keep them warmer and more comfortable. Select

Different styles of **felt-soled wading boots**, including ultralights (left) and midweight (right).

boots that have stiff soles and provide good ankle support.

The choice of felt or rubber soles depends entirely on what sort of surface you'll encounter when you're wading. Felt soles are a must if you are going to be wading in rock- or gravel-bottomed rivers. The felt gives you a good grip on wet and slippery rocks. Rubber-soled boots are good on muddy bottoms. If you plan to be wading out in a lake, for instance, they might be a good choice. For most rivers, however, I recommend felt soles. The felt will eventually wear out with use, but you can "re-felt" your boots with a felt sole kit, which costs about $15.

Lightweight boots, sometimes called *ultralights*, are easier to pack for travel, more affordable, and fine for small streams. The material is not very sturdy, however, and your toes may get beat up from kicking against stones if you use them in rivers with larger rocks.

You can buy boots with ceramic or metal spikes in the soles to provide you with more traction, or you can purchase overshoes with cleats to go over your regular wading boots. Cleats or spiked boots provide more security on super-slippery river bottoms; however, I use them only in places where I know the river is slick, because they are heavier to wear and they tear up the riverbed quite a bit more than regular boots. You might want to consult a local fly-fishing shop to find out what is recommended for your area.

VESTS

I'm happy to tell you that the fly-fishing vest is one article of clothing that is just for you! With so many different styles and sizes of vests available, you'll be able to base your choice on your personal preference. Prices range from $30 to $145.

I have often described a fly-fishing vest as a wallet, glove compartment, toolbox, and purse all rolled into one. It is a way to organize and carry with you all your fly boxes, gadgets, and necessities. There are short styles designed to let you wade up to your midriff, but still keep those items in your lower pockets dry. Everything you carry in your vest will be okay if it gets wet, though, except for the flies inside your fly boxes. If your fly boxes should get wet, open them up at the end of the day to let the flies dry out, or else the hooks will rust.

Vests are made of various materials, some heavier and some quick-drying. There are even some vests made completely of mesh for warmer climates. Choose yours for the climate where you'll be spending most of your fishing time. You might want one with a soft, ribbed collar that

A **fly-fishing vest** allows you ready access to lots of small tools and gear.

will not cut into or rub against your neck. For chilly weather, make sure the vest is large enough to be worn over a bulky sweater or sweatshirt. It should fit loosely without encumbering your arm movements.

Velcro closures make getting in and out of the pockets easier than working with snaps or zippers—and you'll want plenty of pockets, including a couple of very large ones for storing fly boxes and sunglasses. My vest has a big pocket in the back, designed for carrying a landing net. But I hang my net on a D-ring sewn onto the back of my vest and use that large back pocket to hold my rain jacket, lunch, and water bottle. The organization of your vest is completely personal, as is the choice of how much you put in it.

An instructor I used to teach with purchased a particular vest because, through research, he determined that it had the largest pocket capacity of any vest on the market. And boy, did he use every cubic inch! I used to love to watch him give a "tour" of his vest because I couldn't believe all the stuff he had in there! Although he had a slight build, in that vest he looked like the Michelin Man. I used to tease him about his overstuffing—until one day when we were out on the river with a group of students, and the felt sole was coming off a student's boot. My friend quickly and quietly pulled out an adhesive that cured that boot in less than five minutes. I never teased him again and always

FLY FLOTANTS

• • • • • • • • • • • • • • • • • • • •

It's best to tie your fly on the leader before applying flotant. You're less likely to drop the fly, and it's easier to tie knots without flotant on your fingers.

- **Paste and gel.** Use sparingly. Gobbing on too much can cause your fly to sink. Massage some paste or gel between your thumb and fingers and then apply it gently to the fly's hackle and tail. Use special care when the weather is warm, because the heat will often cause these forms to liquefy.

- **Liquid.** Apply directly to the fly. Again, use sparingly. Excess liquid will evaporate, but you might want to blow away any excess to make sure.

- **Dry crystals or powder.** With your fly attached to your leader or tippet, place the fly in the container, close the lid lightly (so as not to crimp the leader), and shake. Remove the fly, still attached to the leader, and gently work in the loose crystals or powder. Blow or tap off any excess.

STRIKE INDICATORS

I carry several different types of indicators for different situations (see illustration page 82). Sometimes I favor yarn for its flotability and sensitivity. In more turbulent water I may choose a cork and pick because it keeps floating better than yarn in rough water. I like to use indicators that can be moved up and down the leader and are reusable. Strike indicators cost from $2 to $5 for a package of three or four and usually come in blaze orange or fluorescent yellow. Choose the color you think you'll be able to see better on the water.

- **Cork and pick:** A plastic foam shape that has a hole or slit through which you insert your leader and secure it with a toothpick.
- **Foam stick-on:** A small precut piece of sticky-backed foam that you can press directly on your leader; not reusable.
- **Strike putty:** A biodegradable putty material which can be shaped to any size and molded around your leader.
- **Yarn:** Preshaped puffs of yarn that attach to your leader usually with a slip knot; treat it with flotant.

> **O**ne of the mysteries I used to yearn to unravel was what all those gadgets were that I saw dangling from anglers' vests.

secretly hoped that he would be around for any emergency I might encounter on a fishing trip.

What's in a vest?

One of the mysteries I used to yearn to unravel was what all those gadgets were that I saw dangling from anglers' vests. Some items, I found out, are necessities, and some are just conveniences. You can spend a lot of money on such gadgets, but you certainly don't have to. Start with the basics and add items along the way.

Basic tools

In chapter 3 I listed the tools essential to fly-fishing: a fishing snip, forceps, and zingers to which you attach your most often used small tools. There are some other gadgets that are not essential but can be very useful, especially the various knot-tying tools. They have springs and clips to hold the line, making it easier to grasp and manipulate the finer leaders and tippets.

Those made to assist in tying a clinch knot are probably the most helpful. I sometimes use one when the weather is so cold that my fingers have trouble tying on the fly. I went fishing with one friend who was having difficulty tying her flies to her tippet because she had these long, beautiful nails. They looked great, but they got in the way. The next time we went fishing, I gave her a knot-tying tool, and she was thrilled to be able to tie her knots quickly with ease.

Leaders and tippet

You should carry a variety of leaders and tippet material to use with different fly sizes. The 7½-foot leaders are the most versatile because you can always lengthen or taper them by tying on more tippet. I like to carry both 7½-foot and 9-foot leaders in 4X, 5X, and 6X, and spools of 4X, 5X, 6X, and 7X tippet.

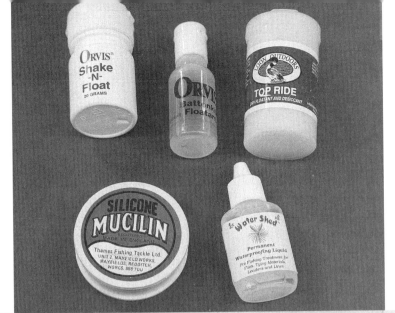

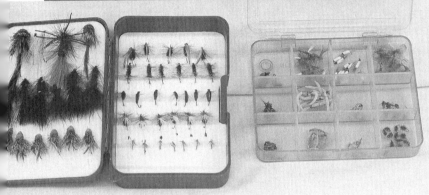

Top: There are lots of different **fly flotants** on the market, including (clockwise from top left) crystals, gel, powder, liquid, and paste. **Above:** Most **fly boxes** feature either foam or compartments to keep flies in place.

Accessories for different fly styles

Depending on whether you are going to fish a dry fly, a nymph, or a streamer, you'll need different accessories to help you.

For dry flies, you should have some kind of flotant. You can experiment with the various forms—gels, waxes, sprays, crystals, or liquids—to find the ones that work best for you. Fly flotants cost between $3 and $6.

If you are going to use nymphs, you'll need either split-shot weights or a product called Shape-a-Weight, which is moldable like clay: you pinch off a small amount and form it around your leader (see photo page 81). You will also need strike indicators to attach to your leader when you fish with a nymph (see photo page 82).

see photo page 81; see photo page 82

RECOMMENDED FLY PATTERNS

Select a few flies in each size. The smaller the number, the larger the fly: a size #12 is larger than a #22.

- **Dry flies** (fished on the water surface): Adams #12 to #22; Adams Parachute #14 to #22; Royal Wulff #14 to #18; Yellow Humpy #12 to #18; Elk Hair Caddis #12 to #16; Stimulator #10 to #14; Rio Grande (or Royal) Trude #14 to #16.

- **Nymphs** (fished underwater): Pheasant Tail #14 to #22; Prince Nymph #10 to #16; Hare's Ear #8 to #12; RS2 Emerger #18 to #22; Miracle Nymph #20 to #24.

- **Wet flies** (fished underwater): Orange Soft Hackle #12 to #16; Leadwing Coachman #12 to #16; Blue Wing Olive Wet #14 to #16.

- **Streamers** (fished underwater): Olive, Black and Yellow Woolly Buggers #8 to #12; Muddler Minnow #10 to #14.

- **Terrestrials** (fished on the water surface): Grasshopper #8 to #14; Red and Black Ant #14 to #18.

VEST-POCKET CHECKLIST

• • • • • • • • • • • • • • • • • • •

Here is a list to review before your fishing outings.

- fishing license
- polarized sunglasses
- fishing snip or a zinger (see page 39)
- hemostats or forceps
- leaders
- tippet
- fly boxes
- flies
- flotant
- weights
- indicators
- knot-tying booklet
- knot-tying tool
- bandanna*
- whistle (see page 125)
- extra set of car keys

*I carry a bandanna in my vest for drying my hands. And on a hot day, nothing feels nicer than dunking that bandanna in the cool water and wiping your face, or putting it around your neck.

When you purchase flies, you are often given a plastic cup with a lid to carry them home in. You can use these cups to store your flies, but I recommend that you purchase a *fly box*. Fly boxes let you keep your flies in one location in your vest instead of having several small containers in different pockets.

Most anglers carry several fly boxes. You can organize your flies by type (a dry fly box and one for nymphs and streamers) or by the different areas you will fish (one box for small streams, another for lakes). Don't feel limited to any particular method. When you first start out, you may need only one box for all your flies.

Fly boxes cost between $2 and $15 and come in several styles. I prefer the ones with foam into which you stick your flies, which is an advantage if you ever drop your fly box. There are also boxes with compartments, which are nice for storing dry flies without crushing them, although the flies in any one compartment sometimes get wadded up and tend to stick to each other.

Loading a vest

When you are ready to put items in the pockets, always put your vest on. You want to get used to putting things away while you are wearing the vest so you'll remember where they are. Try to make a practice of putting the items back in the same pockets each time. Far too often I see anglers rifling through their vests for minutes. This happens to me, too, especially if I haven't been out fishing for a while. Don't worry, it won't take you long to get oriented again, and you will soon reach for items in your vest out of habit versus searching through every pocket.

The most used items, such as fly boxes, flotant, and tippet, should be kept in the easiest-to-reach pockets on the outside front of the vest. In your vest, perhaps you have a wide, flat pocket that will hold all of your leaders together in one spot. Things that you may use only once—sunscreen, first-aid supplies, and lunch—can be stored in the pockets on the back of the vest.

ALTERNATIVES TO A VEST

Some anglers do not like the feel and weight of a vest on their shoulders and backs, and prefer to carry their tackle in a *fanny pack*, *chest pack*, or *waist pack*. I usually prefer to wear a vest, but for fishing a small stream or creek I sometimes travel lighter, wearing a small waist pack or a *lanyard*. A lanyard is a cord or leather necklace that has six to eight swivel hooks to which you can attach flotant, hemostats, and other gadgets.

A chest pack or waist pack designed for fly-fishing has special features for the angler. Custom pockets and loops help you keep things

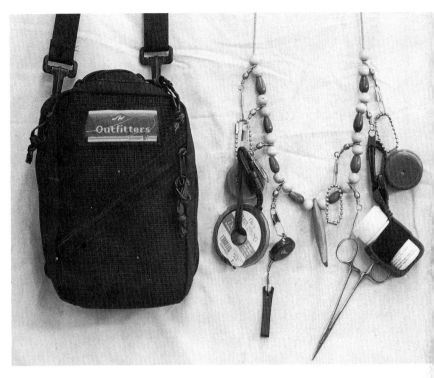

A **chest pack** (left), waist pack, or **lanyard** (right) is a handy alternative to a fly-fishing vest.

organized rather than putting them all in one large pocket. Many fly-fishing waist packs have built-in retractors to which you can attach snips or hemostats, and pockets designed to hold fly boxes. Fly-fishing chest and waist packs have straps that go around your body or neck or clip to the front of your waders.

Fly-fishing chest packs cost from $40 to $120. Before making a choice between a vest and a pack, you might want to talk to other fly fishers about how they organize their tackle. Feel free to try different systems to find out what works best for you. If you wear a fanny pack, though, be careful not to wade in too deep, or your pack and its contents will get soaked.

Although a landing net isn't an essential tool, it will help you capture, unhook, and return the fish to the water more quickly.

LANDING NETS

A net will help you to control the fish at the end of the fight. It's not an essential tool, but if you're releasing your fish, using a net will often enable you to capture, unhook, and return the fish to the water more quickly.

Landing nets range in cost from $15 to $80 and come in various sizes, shapes, and materials. Reasonably priced nets come with lightweight aluminum frames; the

GOIN' FISHING CHECKLIST

• •

As often as I go fishing, I have been known to forget some basic items. I once got to the river with only one boot and had to decide whether to wet-wade in my hiking boots or turn around and go home. The water was cold, but the fishing was great that day!

- fly rod and reel
- both boots
- wading staff (see page 120)
- hat
- sunglasses
- sunscreen
- insect repellent*
- tissue
- first-aid kit (see page 125)
- water filter (see page 127)
- extra shoelaces
- snacks
- bird and plant field guides

- waders
- wading belt
- binoculars
- landing net
- insect seine (see page 139)
- lip balm with sunscreen
- rain jacket
- water bottle
- flashlight
- lighter
- Space blanket
- large trash bags
- pencil and paper
- fishing vest (already packed; see page 114)

*Insect repellent will dissolve leaders, tippet, fly line, and anything else made from plastic! Apply it with the back of your hand instead of with your palm, and make sure it is completely dry before handling your lines. Better yet, rinse your palms and fingers or rub them with dirt before you touch anything plastic.

more expensive ones are handcrafted from beautiful exotic woods such as bird's-eye maple and teak. Choose a size to accommodate the largest fish you're likely to catch. A net to land steelhead can hold a 35-inch fish but would certainly be overkill for 12-inch trout. Long-handled nets are convenient when you fish from a boat or float tube (see chapter 8). Teardrop-shaped nets cut through fast water currents most effectively.

A cotton or nylon net bag, rather than plastic is a must if you are releasing your fish. Hard plastic net bags cause abrasion to the fish's body, removing the protective layer of mucus without which the fish will be susceptible to infection and disease. For catch-and-release fishing, choose a net bag made of knotted cotton or nylon mesh, and make sure to wet both your net and your hands before landing your catch, again to protect the fish's body.

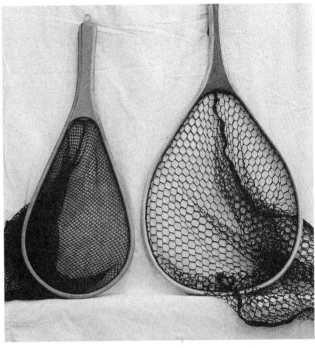

Teardrop-shaped landing nets come with bags in a variety of materials.

PUTTING IT ALL TOGETHER

When I go fishing, I put all my gear in a backpack (or you could also use a duffel bag). It keeps everything in one place in the car and gives me the option of hiking to more remote places to fish. If I think I'll be walking more than half a mile, I also carry all of my fishing togs and change into them at streamside. I hike in comfortable regular clothes, and I wear sturdy hiking shoes in order to have good traction on land, as well as to preserve the felt soles of my wading boots. It's more comfortable hiking in clothes than in fishing gear.

In my backpack, in addition to my vest, waders, wading belt, and boots, I carry a rain jacket, first-aid kit, water bottle, flashlight, extra shoelaces, a lighter, a Space blanket, snacks, and large trash bags. The plastic bags have many uses, from picking up streamside garbage to covering your gear if it rains to having a place to store muddy boots at the end of the day. I also take along a pair of binoculars, and bird and plant identification books. Although I have been accused of having far too much stuff in my pack, part of my enjoyment is in being able to learn about my surroundings. If you want to travel lighter, of course, you can use a small day pack.

For every gadget or piece of tackle different manufacturers offer many choices—and every

• •

Experiment and have fun in all aspects of this sport, from various techniques all the way to tackle. Remember that there are no absolute answers in fly-fishing. Take the eclectic approach and then keep what works for you.

• •

year there are new gadgets to buy and try. Here's where the fun comes in. You'll find products you like and others you don't care for. Experiment and have fun in all aspects of this sport, from various techniques all the way to tackle. Remember that there are no absolute answers in fly-fishing. Take the eclectic approach and then keep what works for you.

Chapter 7

PERSONAL SAFETY AND OUTDOOR SKILLS

WADING

Many women that I have worked with have been concerned about wading in the water. Certainly, river currents can be deceptively strong, and we all should respect the power of moving water. But safety limits in wading are subjective: what seems dangerous to me may be no big deal to someone

Trust your inner voice of reason. And don't let others talk you into anything, especially when wading.

else. Everyone has her own comfort level. I have one friend who I think of as a kamikaze wader! I have seen this woman up to her armpits in water, playing and landing fish after fish. She is completely confident, and I have often just stared in disbelief as she fishes in water levels and currents that make me extremely uncomfortable.

However, in most situations you will not need to get into water more than midthigh deep. And if your comfort level is only midshin—well, you get to set your own rules. Wearing chest waders does not mean that you can or should go into water up to your chest! Remember that the deeper you wade, the more buoyant you will become, making each step seem like walking on the moon. If you begin to feel weightless, work your way slightly downstream, going with the current toward the more shallow ground by the shore.

A good rule of thumb is not to wade into the water unless you have to!

A **wading staff** to help you cross a river can be as simple as a sturdy branch or as sophisticated as a lightweight, collapsible staff made for the purpose.

Chest-high waders provide security if you stumble or fall, even in shallow water: you'll get less water in them—or sometimes none at all—than you would in hip waders. In chest waders you can also squat or kneel down in shallow water without getting your seat wet or having water rush down your legs. Although I almost always wear chest waders, usually I fish standing in water no more than knee deep. Many times I am not even standing in the water.

If you go wading in waders, it is paramount that you also wear a *wading belt* (see chapter 6 on waders). You might want to consider using a *wading staff* as well. This can be as simple as a sturdy branch or stick that you find along the river. Or you can buy a collapsible wading staff made of lightweight aluminum that folds up like a tent stake and fits in a holster hooked to your wading belt. Some anglers remove the basket from a ski pole and use that. Any staff works as a third leg would; it works the same way as putting a hand down instinctively when you feel unstable on your feet. (It's important not to get overconfident, though: a staff doesn't make you invincible.)

You can also use your wading staff as a "feeler" pole. Sometimes it's difficult to see how deep the water is, especially when it is slightly murky. I have used my wading staff to test for water depth and bottom obstructions a few feet ahead before deciding whether it's safe to take that next step.

Wading safely

A good rule of thumb is not to wade into the water unless you have to! I catch most of my fish standing in knee-deep water or in no water at all, even though I'm wearing waders. If you need to go into the water, find a comfortable and stable stance before you begin to fish. If you are unsteady just trying to stand in the water, you are not going to feel comfortable trying to cast or to play a fish from that position.

Don't be in a hurry. To take each step, make sure that one foot is firmly planted before moving the other. Take small shuffle steps by sliding your feet instead of lifting them. I find it helpful to point my knees slightly upstream into the current, and just as in other sports I am ready for action with knees slightly bent and weight shifted forward

Don't, as I once did, let peer pressure talk you out of what you know are your wading limits.

Stand sideways in current, with the water breaking on the side of your leg, for the most stable stance.

to the balls of my feet, not back on my heels. Stand so that the water breaks on your hip or the side of your leg rather than around your seat or lap. Try to cross a river or creek at a downstream angle; it will be a lot easier with some current helping you along. Wading directly upstream against the current is difficult and fatiguing.

Don't, as I once did, let peer pressure talk you out of what you know are your wading limits. I was out on a fly-fishing excursion with three big, strong, tall men, each weighing over 180 pounds. The water was quite high and fast, and I would never have crossed that river on my own. But they all wanted to, so I went along with them. Fortunately, we were using the *buddy system*, grasping one another's shoulders to provide more stability. Even so, I barely made it across the river.

All day as we continued to fish on the other side, the water level was slowly creeping up. When it was finally time to go back, I had only one man to help me, and we were wading side by side, not using the buddy technique. We were almost to the shore when I stepped into a trough I hadn't seen, and off I went, bobbing down the river, panicked. Luckily, my friend was carrying his rod in a rod case and swung it out to me. I grabbed on, and he saved me from being swept downstream.

Looking back, I know I had no business going across that river in the first place! I had been uncomfortable at the thought and should have listened to myself. Trust your inner voice of reason. And don't let others talk you into anything, especially when wading. There are plenty of places to fish, and contrary to popular belief, the fishing isn't always better on the other side. These days, I fish "my own river" and find water that is manageable and comfortable for me.

BUDDY WADING

I use the buddy wading system a lot when I am teaching and guiding. I firmly grab onto the vest or shoulder of my buddy with one hand and ask her to grab mine. We carry our rods in our free hands. We then cross rivers linked together and take turns taking steps. I hope that if I have one foot up, my buddy will have at least one foot down. We serve as each other's anchor. Together we provide a larger, heavier, and more stable means of resisting the current, and we each have someone to hold onto if either of us loses her footing or stumbles. Although any buddy is better than none, I find the biggest buddy I can. You can use two buddies to provide even greater stability.

Buddy wading.

What to do if you fall

> Luckily, many times falls or stumbles in the water result in nothing worse than getting your arms wet or banging up your knees as you try to right yourself again.

Everyone says, "don't panic!" but believe me, you will! Luckily, many times falls or stumbles in the water result in nothing worse than getting your arms wet or banging up your knees as you try to right yourself again. It will be instinct for you to try to get up as quickly as possible. But if the current begins to take you down the river, get your feet downstream of you as soon as you can, and float on your back or seat, facing downstream. River currents naturally push water and objects toward the banks, so you will eventually come to a place where you can stand up and regain your footing. As a precaution, before wading in always be aware of what the river structure looks like downstream from you. It's also a good idea to avoid wading directly above any dangerous obstacles such as drop-offs, fast whitewater, plunge pools, or waterfalls, or where you can see deep water being pushed under large rocks.

If you fall, you will likely get some water down your waders, even if you are wearing a wading belt. Keep in mind that water seeping into your waders will not drag you under, as once thought. You will find that your wading belt will trap air in your legs, allowing you to remain buoyant like a cork. Keep in mind, however, that the weight of water in your waders might make it more difficult to climb back to dry land—although in all the times I've been out fishing, I have never actually taken on more than two cups of water from a fall.

Finally, always remember to think of your own safety first instead of trying to save your fly rod or other gear. Although it's costly, you can always buy more equipment, but you cannot put a price on your own safety.

FEELING SAFE AS A WOMAN

When you go fishing, you may not see many other women out there, and that can be a bit intimidating. But the more you go, the less of an issue it becomes. You soon get used to being perhaps the only woman on the riverbank or lake, and for most women I've talked with, the fishing becomes the primary focus.

As women, however, we are all aware of hazards in today's world. Being safe while fishing is something we all need to consider, but don't let being a woman become a barrier to getting out. A dear friend of mine has a saying that has helped me face a number of challenges in life: "feel the fear, and do it anyway."

When I first went fishing on my own, I was extremely sensitive to the fact that I was the only woman out there on the river, but I was soon put at ease by the other anglers I met. Approaching them with my guard up, ready to assert myself as a woman angler, I was pleasantly surprised to find the conversation focused on fishing or sometimes the weather: "How's your luck? What flies are working? Isn't this a beautiful day?" I remember being astonished at first, but I've found this kind of dialogue especially common in waters regulated for fly-fishing only or for catch-and-release fishing. Anglers you will meet there tend to concentrate on fishing and have little or no interest in anything else, particularly in hassling you about being a woman.

Even so, you may run across some individuals who give you unwanted attention. As women we have learned to take stock of our surroundings, remaining cautious of others on our afternoon walks or runs, or choosing alternate bike routes if we don't like the look of a certain corner or crowd. The same awareness applies when we are fishing. I try not to let thoughts of threat and paranoia enter my mind, but I am as aware of reading my surroundings as I am of reading the water for fish.

We all have different levels of independence. Some will always want to fish with someone else, and the buddy system is certainly one way to feel safe. It's always a good idea to have another person with you so that you can look out for each other. A portable phone can also help in emergencies, though some fishing locations will be out of range. But even if you have a fishing buddy or a portable phone, always be aware of who's out on the water with you. Most of the individuals you encounter will be a lot like you, fly fishers with their attention focused more on the fish than on bothering other people. If you do meet someone who makes you feel uncomfortable, physically leave the area or move to a location that puts another person or two between you and the bothersome individual.

Remember to keep your cool. It isn't worth ruining your fishing day over a piece of water. I was once fishing with a friend on a popular section of river. We were the only two anglers there, and we were enjoying a favorite winter pool we named Tabasco because it's such a hot spot. I had just moved upstream and established myself in another run when I saw a car pull up and park. Two men got out, gathered their gear, and waded out to a spot not more than 20 feet from where I was casting to a fish. I threw them a dirty look that went

"Returning from visiting my sister, I couldn't resist a detour to one of my favorite fishing spots. The decision to stop is not always easy when you're a woman fishing alone, but it was late August, the weather was too beautiful to deny, and the place was deserted. As I readied my equipment, I thought about my great relief at finding this stretch of river vacant. It was more than just having it to myself. It was also about feeling safe off the road alone and perhaps about being relieved of the intimidation I feel as a woman sharing the river with other fishermen. These concerns followed me down the bank as I headed toward the rock outcropping that formed a perfect pool. That's when I saw the fish rising, and I traded in all my worries for a caddis fly and a sweet spot on the water."

—Chris Hill, age 50

EMERGENCY SUPPLIES

I'm always prepared to spend the night if I have to, though I never have. Here's a list of things you may want to keep in your car, just in case:

- water
- jumper cables
- blanket
- sleeping bag
- duct tape
- small shovel
- extra warm clothes
- extra socks and sturdy shoes
- rain gear
- waterproof matches
- candle
- snack food

Remember to keep your cool. It isn't worth ruining your fishing day over a piece of water.

completely unnoticed, so after catching the fish I was working on, I reeled in my line and went back downstream. Sure enough, a few minutes later they followed me! I lost my cool. I began loudly explaining that my friend and I were fishing this spot first and would appreciate it if they would find their own piece of river.

It was ugly. I've replayed that situation in my mind countless times and thought about how I could have handled it better. First, I should have told them at the start that I was working on a fish and asked them if they would please fish an area either upstream or downstream instead of right where I was standing. Then, when they followed me, I should have said that I was working downstream, and would they mind working upstream or at least skipping a few runs to let me have some room. The whole altercation ruined my fishing mood for the next few hours, and looking back, I see that the entire situation just wasn't worth getting so worked up about. I was wrong. They probably didn't know any better, and I should have taken some time to educate them politely instead of losing my temper (see the following section on stream etiquette).

Besides, you never really know who you are getting into a fight with and what they might do. If you try courtesy and someone still refuses to listen, or the situation starts to escalate, learn to just walk away.

Where you choose to fish is another safety consideration. If you're concerned about anyone bothering you or being a threat, consider fishing where help is near instead of in more remote locations. There are many good spots alongside roads, with houses or businesses in sight. Be smart about the time of day as well. As enthusiastic as I am about the sport, I rarely

When I fish alone, I always make sure I have emergency supplies in my vehicle and my vehicle is in good running order.

fish alone after dark. How much of this is being smart versus paranoid? We must each answer that for ourselves.

When I fish alone, I always make sure I have emergency supplies in my vehicle and my vehicle is in good running order. I keep an extra car key and house key safely pinned to the inside of my vest. It's easy to misplace car keys in the excitement of getting ready to fish, and I've been known to lock my keys inside my car. I also keep spare change in the car in case I need to make a call from a pay phone. If I'm going far, I usually let someone know my plans. And among all my other gadgets I also carry a whistle. Your voice will not be heard very far above the sound of rushing water, whereas a whistle can be heard for quite a distance.

I know many women who, whether they fish alone or with others, carry some sort of weapon: a firearm, a knife, or pepper spray. Again, it's a question of what you need to feel comfortable. You don't have to carry a weapon if you don't want to. Your security might be as simple as taking a self-defense course or choosing not to fish in certain areas. Mostly, be aware, look, listen, and trust your intuition.

One woman told me about having gone alone to a remote location. While she was getting her gear ready, she heard a car. Not sure who might be coming her way, she ducked into the bushes and waited. Two men got out of their car and began looking around. Noticing that they weren't dressed for hiking or fishing, she stayed hidden. Eventually they got back into the car and drove away. After waiting several minutes, she came out of her cover and went on to fish, though keeping alert for any other passersby. Who knows what these people were doing out there? Perhaps they were prospecting good spots for later fishing, or innocently looking for a lost dog. You may never find yourself in a threatening situation, but it's always best to stay alert and aware.

STREAM ETIQUETTE

There are some unwritten rules of fishing etiquette, though I've found that common sense is usually the key. Unfortunately, common sense isn't so common anymore, so here are some general guidelines.

FIRST-AID KIT

If you're going to be spending any time in remote areas that are far from immediate response from emergency medical services, it's a good idea to be certified in CPR and first aid. I always carry a first-aid kit with me when I'm guiding and when I'm fishing.

The American Red Cross recommends the following items for a well-stocked first-aid kit:

- Band-Aids
- gauze pads and roller bandages
- waterproof first-aid tape
- Neosporin (antiseptic ointment)
- cold pack
- plastic bags
- disposable gloves
- hand cleaner
- Space blanket
- triangular bandage
- activated charcoal
- syrup of ipecac
- tweezers
- scissors
- small flashlight

Some additions I recommend are bug repellent and sunscreen. Include any personal items such as tampons, any medications you require, and emergency phone numbers.

Be considerate when sharing a section of water with another angler.

Stream etiquette as it applies to space between anglers often depends on where you are. In remote locations like Montana, if there are fifty miles of water to fish and I see only two cars, I may give those anglers several miles of river before I pick a section of stream. In more popular and heavily fished waters, the amount of space to give other anglers is not as clear. Novice fly fishers ask how close is considered too close. The rule of thumb is to get only as close to another angler as you would feel comfortable having someone come close to you.

Also mentally give other anglers some room to work either upstream or downstream. Instead of measuring in yards or feet, I like to allow another angler some fishable water with runs or pools. I will often ask the other angler, "Are you working up- or downstream?" and then I ask, "Do you mind if I work the opposite way?" I have always said yes to anyone who asked my permission to fish nearby; it's the fly fishers who just charge right in without asking that get to me.

When you are passing someone along the river, try to get out of the water if at all possible and pass as far behind that angler as you can. Be sure not to cast your shadow on the water or on the rocks, and try to make the minimum amount of disturbance in the water or on the rocks as you walk. A moving shadow or vibration caused by splashing or kicking a rock will instantly scare fish and put them down very quickly; they may not feed again for several hours.

You can usually tell if other anglers want to chat by whether they make eye contact or not. Most fly fishers I've met stop and take a minute to talk, sharing information and what flies and strategies are working. Use your intuition to recognize an angler who is too focused to talk with you, and just pass by quietly.

I often yield to people who seem completely unaware of fishing etiquette. I would rather not be around to be annoyed by inconsiderate anglers. There are plenty of places to find fish, so I use these times to relocate to a different section of the river, maybe one I've never fished before.

PERSONAL COMFORT

When nature calls

Unless you are fly-fishing near a campground or picnic area you will have to make do with a comfortable rock or grassy bank to eat your lunch and a tall bush to relieve yourself. If no formal rest rooms are available, the good news is that there are informal rest rooms everywhere. I always carry tissue in my vest.

I once fished with a friend on a river that looked like a silver ribbon winding its way through the grassy plain. There were no trees or even bushes; you could see for miles in every direction. I'd had several cups of coffee during the long drive to the river, so I decided I had better relieve myself before putting on my waders. I looked all around and decided it was safe to do so right there alongside the parking lot. Just as I had everything pulled down, a lone car, the only one for miles, drove by. Mercifully, the driver was a woman, who just waved at me while she and my friend were laughing.

When you relieve yourself, make sure to hold onto your wader straps or suspenders and don't let them dangle. That way, you won't have to rinse them off in the river after you're done.

Precautions at high altitudes

Throughout the day, you want to make sure to drink plenty of water, especially if you are fishing at high altitudes. The climate in mountain areas is often very dry, and although you may not feel it, your body will be losing much-needed fluids. I used to carry in all the water I'd need for a day and ration it carefully. Now I carry one bottle of water, in my vest, plus a small backpacker's water purifier. It has replaceable filters that remove 99.9 percent of the impurities. Take care when you are filling your water bottle that you don't splash unfiltered water into it. You should never drink unfiltered stream or lake water because it may be contaminated by animal or human waste.

Remember to slow your pace in the mountains and don't push yourself. Your body will adjust to a higher altitude with time. If you feel the symptoms of altitude sickness—fatigue, dizziness, shortness of breath, and headaches—stop and find a shady, cool place to rest. Drinking water will help alleviate most of the symptoms, but altitude sickness can be serious; if symptoms persist, seek medical attention.

Use a **water purifier** before drinking from any moving or still water.

Chapter 8

FURTHER ADVENTURES

EXPANDING YOUR ADVENTURES

Keep an open mind as to where and how you can apply your fly-fishing skills.

We are all different in how we want to pursue a new interest. Some of you may want to learn as much as you can on your own by reading, renting videos, or just getting out there to fish. Some may prefer to join a group that has planned activities so you can share fly-fishing with others. Either way, there are all kinds of resources available to you; see chapter 10.

Keep an open mind as to where and how you can apply your fly-fishing skills. Wherever you choose to put what you learn into practice, the methodology of fly-fishing is the same, and so is the basic casting stroke. The techniques, strategies, equipment, and flies you use will change according to where you go and what fish you find, but you can fly fish almost anywhere there is water. Your extended fly-fishing trips can be as simple as staying in a streamside motel or camping near your favorite water, or as exotic as traveling to a tropical destination.

Group trips

Becoming part of a group is a great way to share a fly-fishing adventure. There are fishing organizations with which you can affiliate that often plan group trips or outings, and there are also outfitters that organize group trips to destinations all over the country and abroad.

National organizations

Two major organizations are Trout Unlimited (TU) and the Federation of Fly Fishers (FFF). Both have local chapters that meet monthly to discuss club business, grassroots projects, and trips. All levels of fly fishers are welcome, from beginners to professionals. Trout Unlimited is a national group dedicated to preservation and protection of water resources, specifically fishing waters, both for fly-fishing and for other kinds of fishing. TU spends most of its resources fighting for conservation on the national level. The Federation of Fly Fishers is an international organization dedicated to fly-fishing. FFF too devotes resources to the conservation, restoration, and protection of fly-fishing waters through grassroots projects and education at the local chapter level.

"**W**e were all together looking ahead to an incredible adventure together. Who would know what all could happen. As our plane landed at our destination, I remember having a remarkable feeling of freedom and peace come over me. That feeling stayed with me the whole trip, growing in strength with each passing day."

—Gwen Perkins, age 45

With either of these groups, you can join just the national organization or also affiliate with a local chapter. I have found experiences at both levels fun and inviting. The chapters often organize fishing trips, which makes it easy to get involved. Joining one is a great way to meet others who fly fish and find out a lot about fly-fishing opportunities in your area.

Women's groups

You will likely meet other women anglers who are involved in groups for men and women, but there are also fly-fishing organizations just for women. In 1996 a women's fly-fishing club in California organized the first annual International Festival of Women Fly Fishers (IFWFF) to celebrate women anglers and women's fly-fishing clubs from all parts of the country. The response was overwhelming, and there has been a festival each year since then. IFWFF is held at a different location every year, and fly-fishing women of all levels of ability come together from all over the country to fly fish and get to know one another. There are instructional seminars and interesting speakers on various fly-fishing topics and issues; however, I think one of the main benefits of attending IFWFF is to meet other women who fly fish. The festival attendees range from interested women who have not yet tried the sport to those who are involved as professionals in the fly-fishing industry.

In 1998, the women who attended the 3rd Annual IFWFF voted to establish, in addition to the yearly festival, an organization called International Women Fly Fishers (IWFF) as a resource for women around the country. Because it's so new, the goals and directives of the group are still being formed, but IWFF can already help if you are searching for women's fly-fishing groups in your area. You should also consider attending the annual festival.

A fly-fishing magazine recently listed more than thirty women's fly-fishing clubs and groups across the country, in some twenty different states. The Colorado Women Flyfishers (CWF) is one example. It has more than 100 members statewide and meets monthly for scheduled programs that range from such topics as fly-fishing in salt water to question-and-answer panels. It's great fun to meet other women who live nearby and share your interests, and with whom you can fly fish. The club also organizes a trip to a different fishing destination each month, which makes it easy for everyone to feel included and become involved.

There are also groups for women interested not only in fly-fishing but in such activities as hunting or learning survival skills. An organization called Becoming an Outdoors Woman offers all sorts of outdoor educational programs for women.

If you have trouble finding a group in your own area, consider starting one yourself. One woman told me that she had organized her own fly-fishing club with neighbors that she had met at a newcomers' get-together. When the subject had turned to fishing, the group decided to plan monthly excursions with their families for potluck picnics and fly-fishing.

Outfitters and guides

> Good guides are there to help even a beginner better her skills and knowledge.

Another way to expand your adventures is by going to a fly-fishing lodge or taking a trip with a fly-fishing outfitter. The great thing about going with outfitters is that they do all the planning and provide not only the rods and tackle but often horses or drift boats to take you to the selected area.

Reel Women Outfitters offers fly-fishing day trips and multiple-day outings: floating local rivers in a boat, fly-fishing for bonefish in the Bahamas, horseback trips to pristine wilderness waters. All the guides are experienced, with diverse backgrounds in fly-fishing. A trip with Reel Women Outfitters offers a unique opportunity for a woman angler of any ability to travel to world-class fishing destinations, both in the western states and abroad.

Hiring a guide or an outfitter for a fishing trip is another great way to learn new skills and improve techniques. I tell clients that hiring a guide is like having a private as opposed to a group lesson. The going rate for a one-day guide trip ranges from $200 to $350 for two anglers, depending on whether you choose walk-and-wade fishing or a float trip (see pages 131–32). When I was first learning, the thought of hiring a guide was intimidating and somewhat embarrassing because I felt that I wasn't good enough. On the contrary! Good guides are there to help even a beginner better her skills and knowledge. A good guide is a teacher and buddy who shares knowledge and experience freely. A guide should never make you feel ignorant or clumsy. When you hire a guide, he or she is working for you, not personally fishing on your nickel.

If it's your first time hiring a guide or using a guide service, ask questions. What is the typical day like? How many anglers does the fee cover? How long can you expect to be on the water? Do you need your own equipment, or will the guide supply everything? Are there additional charges for flies or tackle? Is tipping customary? What other items or gear should you bring?

The guides I know and have worked with have a contagious enthusiasm and passion for fly-fishing that they are eager to share. They are patient and will work at whatever pace is comfortable for you, rather than push clients to satisfy their own fishing agenda. If you want to learn different techniques or work on improving your casting, they will help you. A common belief is that a guide is there to ensure you get fish. Certainly, hooking fish can be a highlight of the day, but don't consider it the primary reason you're out there. Your attitude should be one of learning, and a guide should be there to explain and teach you enough so that you can eventually be successful on your own. Ask questions and try to understand the different line setups, presentations, techniques, and why your guide has selected a certain type of water. Most of all, enjoy yourself!

Of course, there are good guides and outfitters, and ones that aren't so good; most have a reputation for being one or the other. As in any business, word of mouth is the best source for a referral. If you want to hire a guide for a specific area or river, ask around among fly-fishing groups in that area or inquire at local fly-fishing shops. (For more on outfitters and lodges, see chapter 10.)

> **M**ake sure you clarify with the guide how many anglers the fee covers. For example, a guide might charge $230 for either one or two anglers but charge an extra $100 if a third angler goes along.

> **C**ast from a drift boat while standing in the front of the boat. If there are two anglers in the boat, one stands in the front and the other stands behind the person at the oars.

Float trips

If you enjoy canoeing, rafting, or kayaking, then I envy you your first fly-fishing float trip! You'll never think about all that beautiful water in the same way again. A boat provides great access to all kinds of fishing opportunities. A good friend who was already a fly-fishing guide decided to expand his skills and become a whitewater rafting guide. He said he learned to look at water very differently from a rafting point of view, but although he enjoyed his new perspective, he just couldn't stand to be floating by so much great fly-fishing water without fishing it. Eventually he recruited clients to fly fish from the raft.

You *can* fly fish from a raft, but most watercraft fly-fishing on a river is done from a *drift boat*. A drift boat is wide with a high bow for stability.

Fly-fishing from a **drift boat** is another way to expand your fishing experience.

ONE MISTY MORNING

· · · · · · · · · · · · · · · · · · ·

I woke up really early, even before the sun. It had rained the night before, and fog shrouded the lake. It was so wonderfully gray, I could not even wait for coffee. I was dressed and climbing in my belly boat in record time. The fog was so dense, visibility was only about twenty feet. I could see the silent rings forming on the calm surface of the water around me. There was a hatch of tiny midges, and the fish were eating as if they knew every sound would be magnified by the fog. So dainty, so quiet.

I find the smallest fly in my box and cast the little guy out there. A perfect landing, three little rings, then calm. I watch as shreds of mist drift between me and my fly. I am patient, hoping my deception works. Then suddenly it's gone and only a ring is left. I set the hook, and the calm is broken. It will not be the biggest fish I've ever caught, but it might be the most magic. I know I want another day like this.

—Chris Hill, age 50

It has no motor; propulsion and steering are done the old-fashioned way, by means of oars. Fly-fishing from a drift boat is a wonderful experience. You feel so free, you see a lot of beautiful landscape, and with a skilled person at the oars you are able to cast anywhere. One of the things about fishing is that you always think that you want to be fishing the other, usually inaccessible bank just as the grass always looks greener on the other side. With a boat, you can access that other side! (For more about fly fishing from a drift boat, see chapter 10.)

Float tubes and pontoon boats

A *float tube*, sometimes called a *belly boat*, consists of an inflated inner tube covered with a nylon outer shell to which a mesh seat is attached. A separate inflatable backrest serves as both a cushion and a safety flotation device. A float-tuber wears waders to keep dry and fins for propulsion. A float tube is like having your own personal boat, complete with built-in pockets for your lunch and gear. Although you can wear a short fishing vest that won't let your lower pockets get wet, when I float-tube I don't wear a fishing vest at all but store my stuff in the float tube pockets.

Float tubes can be either U-shaped or O-shaped. The "U-boats" are easier to get in and out of, but a round one will support greater weight. Float tubes are used primarily in still water (although some places recommend and allow their use in rivers), where they give you access to the entire pond or lake, not just the shore areas that are clear of brush and other obstacles. Casting from a float tube can be challenging because you are casting while

Float tubes can be either **O-shaped** (left) or **U-shaped** (right).

Fly-fishing a
pond from
a U-shaped
float tube.

BOATS AND WATER CLASSIFICATION

• • • • • • • • • • • • • • • • •

Some pontoons can be used only on still water, and other larger ones can be used on both still water and moving water. From a boating perspective, moving water is categorized on a six-point scale from class 1 to class 6, with 6 the most difficult water to navigate. Manufacturers of pontoon boats will specify the highest degree of difficulty or class of moving water recommended for a specific pontoon. If you plan to use a pontoon on any moving water, according to Greg Felt, owner of Canyon Marine Whitewater Expeditions and co-owner of ArkAnglers (Salida, Colorado), "Know your ability, know your limits, and don't boat alone."

sitting in the water, so it's easy to let your line touch or slap the water in your back cast—which is not desirable. Think of keeping your back cast high off the water. You might also want to consider purchasing a 10-foot rod because its greater length will help you keep your back casts and false casts off the water. You can also let your line trail along in the water as you kick with your fins, a bit like trolling from a boat.

Like float tubes, *pontoon boats* also use inflated inner tubes, but the pontoon has two, attached with a frame. Again, you wear waders and fins, though the frame allows you to sit higher out of the water, which makes casting a little easier. In larger pontoons, oars are attached to the frame for greater maneuverability. The idea is that the pontoon lets you move in different locations, beach the craft, and then walk-and-wade fish. Or you can fish from the pontoon as it drifts downstream.

PREGNANCY AND OTHER SPECIAL PHYSICAL CONDITIONS

A fellow instructor who was teaching a beginning class had a student with only one arm. Though the student was concerned that he would not be able to cast or play a fish, he had always wanted to fly fish. With a little instruction about ways to handle the equipment to suit his needs, he went on to hook, play, and land a nice rainbow trout on his own.

If you are physically challenged, you too might have to handle equipment differently to suit your needs. If access to the water is a concern, find a place where a river or lake shore has a gradual slope. I know of two areas on different sections of a river that allow access if you are chairbound. Perhaps fishing from a float tube or boat where you can work from a sitting position is an option. The point is, if you have the desire to fly fish and perhaps a bit of creativity, there are ways.

Once when my dad and I were getting our lines ready to fish, a van pulled up and parked. We watched as a ramp

Fly-fishing from a **pontoon boat**.

THE FAMILY THAT FISHES TOGETHER . . .

Searching for a sport that I should enjoy with my husband and children, I tried baitfishing and found that it did not move me at all. I would sit on the shore with that pole of mine and be as bored as a woman could be. Eventually I refused to go fishing with my family.

Then one afternoon my former boss agreed to take three of us—women who had never held a fly rod and had not the foggiest idea what to do with one—to try our luck at fly-fishing. After he explained the basics to us, I waded into the cold creek with bare feet and found a spot and stayed there, even though it was mid-October. Several other anglers watched our antics in amusement as my boss ran back and forth, teaching each of us to cast and roll the line, helping us time and time again until we caught on. With each cast I found I had more and more control over the line. This was what I had been searching for. This kind of fishing kept my interest.

What's more, it gave me something in common with my 16-year-old son, Daniel, who had begun fly-fishing about a year earlier. After my experience with my boss, Daniel and I went out late one evening to a stream a couple of miles from our home. I was still pretty new to every aspect of this game, but I treasure the memory of my time with Daniel—the sound of the creek, the sunset against the mountains, and the smile on my son's face. He was very successful that day, catching fish after fish while I caught willows and sagebrush. Yet even tied up in the willows, I knew I had found two things in my life: a new interest and the patience to pursue it (years before, I would have cut that line and demanded to be taken home).

Now, I urge every woman to learn the art and joy of fly-fishing. Take advantage of classes offered in your area, or have a good friend show you the ropes. I guarantee you'll be hooked.

—Martha Rodriguez Thompson, age 38

came down and a man in a wheelchair worked his way out. With his rod strapped across his chair, he rolled down the gradual slope of the riverbank and went right into the water. I was somewhat alarmed, wondering if he would need help, but my alarm soon turned to delight as he accessed the water with skill and ease. He cast and fished from the wheelchair, appearing comfortable and confident. I remember thinking, "why not?" It's often only the limitations of our mind-set that keep us from making the "impossible" possible.

And, yes, you can fly fish while pregnant. Your main challenge might be finding a set of waders to fit comfortably. Or you can fish without wearing waders. The friend I mentioned in chapter 1, who was anticipating the birth of her first child, refused to be deterred by her family's concern about her "condition." On a nice, warm afternoon, two weeks before going into labor, she declared that she wanted to get out of the house and go fly-fishing for a few hours. I was a bit shocked at first and then delighted to help her into an oversized pair of waders and drive her to a nearby pond for an adventure in float tubing. The cool water was a welcome change from the afternoon sun, and there she was, kicking along in the water with a pair of fins, shrieking in delight as she caught fish after fish.

Your own interest in fly-fishing can be contagious to children, and you might find yourself catching some of their enthusiasm in return.

FLY-FISHING WITH CHILDREN

I have a special place in my heart for children who are interested in fly-fishing and in learning with family or a family friend. It comes from my own experiences with my grandparents, dad, and brother. Another woman told me, "I remember fishing with my grandfather, many years ago, and feeling the freedom of it all and the thrill when I caught one. There's nothing like it." It's wonderful to see a parent or relative bringing a child into the fly shop so they can look around together, or an adult fly fishing with a child on the river.

The key is togetherness. Fly-fishing kept a bond between my dad, brother, and me when I was growing up and still does. A great excuse like fly-fishing can manage to reunite us as a family, even when time is so limited and time off from work so cherished. I will fly almost anywhere, anytime, to have a chance to fly fish with my family.

There are classes especially for parents and children who want to learn to fly fish together. In many ways, it's easier when both parent and child are both new to the sport and neither is the expert. We have had children as young as eight and as old as forty-something come with a parent to learn to fly fish.

SHOW, DON'T TELL

Late one morning, my daughters Michelle and Kierie and I hiked 12 kilometers to a meadow beside a stream. We had waited out lightning and rain from the edge of a thunderstorm and arrived just as the gale-force winds of the front subsided and a magic hour settled on the valley. The girls sat down to eat their lunches. They were laughing at my attempts to tease the fishes with every variety of nymph and dry fly in my box until, in the frenzy of a fly hatch, I hooked a giant cutthroat. The two of them flew from their picnic spot in the grass to the edge of the creek without touching the ground. Kierie freed the "big one" from a tangle in the net and nursed him back to sensibility. She set him free and took my fly rod. Michelle was searching through my box of flies to make the next selection.

—Shari McMahon, age 45

It seems that children do best if they are at least eight years old, although a lot depends on the individual child. I'll never forget author Barry Reynolds's photo of his son when he was four, holding up a bluegill or a crappie that he had caught on a fly rod. What I remember about that picture is not the fish but the look on his boy's face, beaming with delight. For most kids under age eight or ten, however, the concepts of casting and presentation are a lot for them to take in, and they may not yet have developed the necessary dexterity. When you are working with children for their first few times, it's important that the kids be successful and that both you and they are having fun. They will soon learn the virtues of patience and perseverance if their instructor is patient and encouraging.

In addition to parent-and-child classes, there are also fly-fishing classes just for children. For example, the local Trout Unlimited chapter in Evergreen, Colorado, works with the public school's outdoor education program, training counselors to teach fly-fishing and fly-tying to fifth-graders. Some local fly-fishing shops also offer classes for children, covering the basics of casting and fly selection, and sometimes fly-tying basics.

It's important that, like adults, children have the opportunity for actual fly-fishing experience within the context of the class. A book I recommend for further reading on the subject is *Fly Fishing with Children*, by Philip Brunquell.

Chapter 9

REAL BUGS, FLIES YOU TIE, AND FINAL THOUGHTS

AQUATIC ENTOMOLOGY

One of my students had a frustrated, almost disgusted look on her face during a discussion in a fly-fishing class. Later I asked her if anything was the matter. Exasperated, she replied, "You mean in order for me to be a fly fisher, I have to be a hydrologist, a fisheries biologist, and an entomologist!?" Well, not exactly, I assured her. She didn't have to be an expert in those studies, but I told her that the more she learned about them, the more successful she would be at fly-fishing. There may be times that you feel like you are back on a fifth-grade field trip, learning about your outdoor environment for the first time. I know I still do! Entomology is the scientific study of insects. As fly fishers, we are not concerned with all insects, just the aquatic ones—those that live at least part of their lives somehow connected with water. In other words, we want to know about the bugs that at some point are simply fish food!

> The more you learn about water, fish, and bugs, the more successful you'll be at fly-fishing.

In any stream or lake, many insects call that water system "home," living in water during their developmental stages. One day, they get the urge to emerge. They work themselves up to the top of the water, where they sprout wings, fly off to swarm in a mating dance, and then return to deposit eggs in the water to start the whole cycle all over again. As fly fishers, we call that wing-

Four insect characteristics are most important to anglers in this order: their size, shape, color, and behavior. Once you know what the fish are used to seeing as food, you can better match your flies or fly patterns to the naturals.

sprouting point in the insects' life cycle a hatch. The joy and beauty of this whole cycle is that during any part of this usually year-long life cycle, these aquatic insects are available to fish as food. As anglers, we can imitate any one of these insects during any stage of its life with an artificial fly: a nymph to imitate a nymph, a wet fly to imitate an emerging adult, and a dry fly to imitate a mature insect with wings. Keep in mind that fish feed almost 90 percent of the time underwater, eating the aquatic nymphs (immature forms of insects) that live in the water and under rocks. The other 10 percent of the time the fish eat adult insects that are floating on top the water.

Some anglers study the habits of aquatic insects intensely in order to be able to tie fly patterns that look and "act" more realistic. Others spend many hours studying the insects themselves, figuring out how and when to fish the appropriate stages. As I told my students, the more you know, the better angler you will become, but rest assured that you do not have to become a bug specialist or learn the habits and Latin names of each insect. Four insect characteristics are most important to anglers in this order: their size, shape, color, and behavior. Once you know what the fish are used to seeing as food, you can better match your flies or fly patterns to the naturals.

As anglers we are fascinated to know what fish view as food. In their underwater environment, they dine on different sizes and shapes of insects and other aquatic life, such as shrimp. Some fish eat large insects, perhaps half the length of your index finger, if they are prevalent. For other fish the most common food source may be only very tiny insects no longer than the width of a pencil. Fish are usually going to be feasting on the most common—not always the largest insects present. As a whimsical parallel, suppose a fish is surrounded by the cocktail peanuts it is used to seeing as food. That fish will probably continue eating peanuts, even if a slice of pizza comes by.

So, in order to imitate their food, we must first find out what the fish are feeding on. To determine what insects are in the water you want to fish, you will learn to be a good observer. As you approach the water and are getting your gear ready, notice what is happening around you. Are insects flying out of the bushes as you walk to the water? Are delicate-looking insects landing on your vest? Birds,

Select a fly most like the aquatic insects in the fishing area.

mainly swallows, swooping down as if to kiss the surface of the water in order to eat an insect, may be showing you that insects are hatching and drifting in the river. All these subtle signs tell you that it might be a good time to tie on a dry fly. If a bug happens to alight on your vest, see if you have a dry fly resembling it in size, shape, and color.

If you don't see any flying or crawling insects, you will probably be more successful with flies that drift under the water's surface. Then the easiest way to determine what fly to use is to flip over a rock in shallow water near the bank. Look to see what may be crawling on the bottom of the rock and then, again, look to see what you may have in your fly box to match the natural creature in size, shape, and color. Don't worry: these aquatic critters may look creepy and crawly, but they don't bite.

Seining

Another method, actually more accurate than flipping rocks, is to seine the river. A *seine* is a screen you hold under the water to collect insects you dislodge from the bottom of the stream or lake. There are many different styles, even some you place over your landing net. They range in price from $10 to $20, or you can make your own for less than $5 by fastening screen mesh purchased at a hardware store to two dowels. A light-colored seine or screen makes it easiest to see the insects.

Place your seine net in the water downstream of your feet and slide your feet around in the water, displacing rocks and stirring up clouds of dirt and debris. Keep your net in the water to catch as much drifting debris as you can. Then quickly pull the net against the current in order to trap all its contents. You will be amazed at what you find— it's a jungle down there! Your seine net should come alive with many different types of insects. If you don't get a good sample, repeat the process in a slightly different location. And try different

Seining a river is another way to identify local fish food and match them to the flies you have on hand.

types of water, as different insects will prefer faster or slower water.

Look carefully at your sample to discover what type and size of insect is most prevalent— not always the biggest, remember, but the most numerous. I like to describe this process as play-

All aquatic insects spend 90 percent of their lives under the water, going through their immature stages of development. We refer to live insects in these stages as *nymphs*, *larvae*, or *pupae* and use artificially tied nymphs, wet flies, and emergers to imitate them.

ing the percentages. If there is one large aquatic worm but 80 percent of your catch is very small nymphs, take out your fly box and look for the closest imitation to those nymphs. In making a match, the most important factor to note is the size of the insect, then the shape, and finally the color. Some people find it hard to believe that even large trout will eat such small insects, but believe me, it's true.

Four main food groups

The hundreds of different aquatic insects, thankfully, can be grouped into four main categories: *stone flies*, *mayflies*, *caddis flies*, and *midges*. Each family has unique features that makes it easy to identify. Among the characteristics they all share, however, is a multistage life cycle. All aquatic insects spend 90 percent of their lives under the water, going through their immature stages of development. We refer to live insects in these stages as *nymphs*, *larvae*, or *pupae* and use artificially tied nymphs, wet flies, and emergers to imitate them. Only about 10 percent of aquatic insects' lives are spent as adults with wings, above and on the surface of the water. During this stage, we use artificially tied dry flies to imitate the adult insects with wings. Most of the hatches occur from spring through late fall, when water temperatures are warmer.

The following description of each "food group" includes a list of artificial flies that imitate those insects. It's a good idea to get familiar with the names of the fly patterns, but instead of memorizing each type of fly and exactly what it's supposed to represent, rely on a variety of sizes. For instance, a #14 or #16 Pheasant Tail Nymph is designed to imitate a mayfly nymph but can also be used to imitate a caddis pupa and, tied in a larger size (say, #12), can imitate a stone fly nymph. Or a Rio Grande Trude, a dry fly attractor pattern (not tied to imitate any one specific adult insect) can be used in different sizes to imitate an adult stone fly, mayfly, or caddis. For each pattern listed, there are dozens of others that will also be effective.

Stone flies

Stone fly nymphs can be recognized by their armadillo-like appearance. They range in size from 3 inches all the way down to about ¼ inch, or about fly sizes #4 to #16. Stone fly nymphs will be the ones most likely to crawl around on or off your seine net. Their legs, antennae, and tails always come in pairs (never more than two tails). You will find them in assorted sizes and in a range of colors from yellow to brown and black. If you have spent time on a creek or river, you may have seen empty stone fly shells or dried shucks stuck to rocks and bridge trestles. Stone fly nymphs don't emerge out of the water but crawl onto rocks and riverbanks, then leave behind their nymphal shucks as they change into their winged adult form. Adults are very clumsy in the air and look bulky and awkward when they fly. At rest, their wings lie flat against their bodies. In size they match dry flies from #4 to #18. Stone flies can live for a few weeks in their winged adult stage. They eventually mate, return to the water to lay eggs, and then die, and the whole cycle begins all over gain.

- **Stone fly nymph patterns:** Golden Stone Fly, Giant Black Stone Fly, Kaufman's Stone, Yellow Bead-Head Stone Fly
- **Stone fly adult patterns:** Stimulator, Sofa Pillow, Madame X

Mayflies

Mayflies are delicate in appearance. The nymphs can be very tiny, from about ¾ inch down to ¹⁄₁₆ inch, or about fly sizes #12 to #24. When you find them in your seine sample, they may look as if they are wilted. Most don't crawl very well but are better as swimmers. A mayfly nymph has two or three tails that often mat together when it is taken out of the water, looking like one thick tail. Adult mayflies also look very delicate. They have upright wings—often described as "sailboats" on the water—and slender, curved, banana-shaped bodies. Of all the insects, mayflies are my favorite because of their graceful and delicate appearance. Adult mayflies match fly sizes #12 to #24 and range in color from yellow and pumpkin to rust, olive, gray blue, and black. Mayflies live as adults for only 24 to 36 hours during which, like the stone flies, they return to the water to lay eggs and die.

- **Mayfly nymph patterns:** Hare's Ear, Pheasant Tail, Baetis Nymph, Prince Nymph
- **Mayfly emerger patterns:** Orange Soft Hackle, RS2 Emerger, Hare's Ear Wet
- **Mayfly adult patterns:** Adams, Pale Morning Dun, Blue Wing Olive, Light Cahill

Caddis flies

Instead of nymphs, the immature forms of the caddis are called *larvae* and *pupae*. Caddis larvae are the most curious to me. They range in size from ¾ inch to about ¼ inch (fly sizes #12 to #18). Some build houses or cases to protect themselves as they mature and some attach themselves by a web under rocks. Different species of caddis build cases out of different materials, like the three little pigs: houses of stone or sticks or decayed leaf and wood matter. Caddis larvae secrete a sort of glue which holds their cases together and attaches them to rocks and sticks. After living underwater for about a year, the larva turns into a pupa, which then shoots up to the surface of the water when it is ready to change into its adult form. Adult caddis flies look like moths with wings that will remind you of a pup tent. Adults match fly sizes #10 to #20 and come in colors ranging from tan to brown to black. You will usually see them hovering above or near water.

- **Caddis larva patterns:** Bead-Head Caddis Larva, Buckskin, Peeking Caddis

- **Caddis pupa patterns:** La Fontaine Sparkle Pupa, Stalcup Bead-Head Caddis Emerger

- **Caddis adult patterns:** Elk Hair Caddis, X Caddis, Stocking Sedge

Midges

Last but certainly not least are the mighty midges. Although they are the tiniest of all the aquatic insects, they make up for their size in their numbers. Midges, like caddis flies, go through a larval and pupal stage; there are no midge nymphs. Midge larvae range from ½ inch down to ¹⁄₁₆ inch, or fly sizes #18 to #26, and look like tiny segmented worms. They can be found in many colors, including cream, olive, tan, and red. When the midge larva becomes a pupa, it has a bulbous area by its head. Adult midges are gnatlike in appearance and have no tails. Unlike all the other aquatic insects, they can be seen flying around water almost every day of the year, even in the dregs of winter. Many anglers don't fish midge hatches, though, because the adults are so tiny, about the size of fly sizes #18 to #26.

- **Midge larva patterns:** String Thing, Miracle Nymph, Blood Midge

- **Midge pupa patterns:** Brassie, Palomino Midge, WD40

- **Midge adult patterns:** Griffith's Gnat, Cannon's Suspender Midge

Other food sources

Aside from the four main food groups of stone flies, mayflies, caddis flies, and midges, other items that make up a fish's diet include aquatic worms, crustaceans such as shrimp (often called scuds) and crayfish, and other small fish—all imitated by flies fished below the water surface—and terrestrial insects such as grasshoppers, beetles, and ants, which are imitated by dry flies. Like aquatic insects, these other fish food forms are matched with artificially tied flies first by size, then by shape and color.

FLY SELECTION

When you're choosing artificial flies in a fly shop, you will find them grouped into the four basic categories of nymph, wet fly, dry fly, and streamer. Nymphs and wet flies, fished underwater, are meant to tumble around with water currents. A nymph imitates a real nymph, pupa, or larva. (The term *nymph* is also used generically to denote all the smaller flies fished below the water, including worm, egg, and shrimp patterns.) Wet flies and emergers, tied to represent insects that are swimming their way up to the surface to sprout wings as adults, are often thought of as being in between a nymph and a dry. Dry flies are a category of flies designed to float on top of the water like a cork. Artificially tied dry flies include the adult forms of aquatic insects or any bug with wings that's supposed to fly. Terrestrials such as grasshoppers and ants are also grouped with dry flies because they also float atop the water. Streamers are long flies that are fished underwater and include patterns to represent minnows and even leeches.

All fly fishers have favorite flies and flies that they swear by when all else fails. You too will find flies that you fish with confidence and have a tendency to favor over others.

Often, however, you will see them tied with bright, gaudy colors such as fluorescent purple, orange, and yellow—they will remind you of a feather boa. Such garish colors often serve to irritate the fish into biting or striking in self-defense out of sheer aggravation. Others are tied in muted colors such as tan and olive to imitate live small fish. Streamers are wonderful flies to use in the spring and fall, when fish are spawning and lots of small fish are likely to be present in the water.

At this point you may be wondering how on earth you can carry enough flies to match all these insects, both nymphs and adults. It's always a good idea to have a variety of fly patterns in both nymph and adult forms in a variety of sizes. But even though it's best to be prepared for everything you might encounter, there are a few good all-around patterns you should always carry with you. All fly fishers have favorite flies and flies that they swear by when all else fails. You too will find flies that you fish with confidence and have a tendency to favor over others. The key is confidence: there are some flies that I know are going to be good because they've worked like a charm in the past. Although I carry more than 80 different patterns in a series of sizes, I admit that I use probably only a dozen patterns a majority of the time. Given the choice, I would rather carry fewer patterns in a wide range of sizes, than fill up my fly boxes with only one size each of many different styles. For instance, I'd choose an Adams, a traditional dry fly, in sizes #12 to #24, over a variety of dry flies all in size #14.

There are some regional differences in fly patterns and particularly in size. I've suggested some essential flies that will cover almost all situations, regardless of where you might be. Still it's always a good idea to consult local fly shops about particular patterns, or specific hatches that may be occurring in the area.

You'll probably always remember the first fish you hook, the first fish you catch on a dry fly, and finally, the first fish you catch on a fly you've tied yourself.

You will want to have at least two of each type and size in your fly box. It's heartbreaking to have just one of a fly that is working like magic and then to lose that one in a bush or a fish's mouth. It's also a good idea to have that extra fly with you when you look for more of the same kind in the fly shop. You'll find, however, that there are individual differences in the ways that one pattern with the same name is tied.

Some may come in a bead-head style or with flashback material to add extra sparkle. You might want to have a few of these variations, in addition to the traditional types, to fish when the water is cloudy or murky. The added weight of the bead-head nymph also helps it sink more quickly.

> Learning to tie flies will give you a greater understanding of natural insects and their behavior in or on the water.

FLY-TYING BASICS

There are certain milestones that you remember as a fly fisher. You'll probably always remember the first fish you hook, the first fish you catch on a dry fly, and finally, the first fish you catch on a fly you've tied yourself: that is, a fly that you have created by wrapping a bare hook with thread, fur, and feathers. Learning to tie your own flies is an art and skill in itself. You may never have the interest or the time it takes to learn, and that's okay. But if you are interested, it can be very rewarding to create with your own hands a fly that's close enough to the real thing to fool a fish. After an initial investment of tools and materials, tying your own can also make your flies more affordable. Instead of spending $2 for a nymph, you can tie one for less than 25 cents.

The best way to get started is to purchase a basic fly-tying kit. A kit costs $45 to $100 and includes an instruction book, tools, hooks, and materials to tie several different fly patterns. The more expensive kits come with tools of better quality and enough materials to tie many more types of flies. The most expensive item in the kit is the fly-tying vise, which securely clamps the hook to which you attach various materials. A Woolly Bugger streamer, for example, may use a kind of feather called maribou for the tail and synthetic chenille in the body. Thread is used to wrap and secure the different parts of the fly.

Fly-tying classes are offered at most fly-fishing shops, or you can get some great instructional books (see chapter 10). I recommend finding one that has color photos depicting step-by-step details for specific fly patterns.

Learning to tie flies will give you a greater understanding of natural insects and their behavior in or on the water. For instance, by tying a beetle with flimsy, black rubber legs that look like pieces cut from rubber bands, you will see that the legs imitate the moving, kicking legs of a live beetle that has fallen helplessly into the water. Your fly-tying knowledge will assist you as an angler because you'll have a better idea of what the flies are supposed to imi-

> Fly-fishing is filled with opportunities, some of them missed, some turned into successes. It's always a learning experience. You never know what is waiting for you around the next bend or behind that next island. Fly-fishing is a journey, a process always filled with hope that you'll get that fish on the line. But don't forget to enjoy the ride along the way.

tate, and a better imitation is more likely to catch fish. As a flytier, you will look at natural insects in a different way, often thinking about how best to use what materials to look like the real thing. It is also great fun to invent your own fly patterns.

FINAL THOUGHTS

You may be wondering how in the world you are ever going to feel proficient in this sport. The best method of learning is to go out there and try. The more times you fly fish, the more you will learn and the more comfortable you will feel.

I recently had an experience that both frustrated and humbled me. Although I have been fly-fishing for some twenty years, my experience has been mainly with trout fishing. So saltwater fly-fishing was a whole new world to me when I got my first opportunity to cast at a small school of twenty to thirty bonefish. I had read the books, seen pictures in magazines, and heard the wonderful stories, and here I was, wading out to the fish in knee-deep salt water.

Suddenly, the school of bonefish turned and started swimming right toward me. They were about 80 feet away and closing fast. My friends began shouting, "Over there to your right! Now there to your left! There! Right in front of you!" I fell apart. Even with all my casting experience, I couldn't get the fly to go out ten feet in front of me. The bonefish were now 50 feet away and coming right at me. My line was all tangled up. Bonefish, 40 feet, still swimming right to me. My hands were shaking so badly I couldn't get my line and fly untangled. Bonefish, 30 feet. I felt faint and realized I was hyperventilating. Bonefish, 25 feet.

Looking back, I think I should have just taken my 9-foot rod and used it like a spear. Those fish got so close that it would've worked! I never even got off one cast before they saw me in the water. They all turned, churning up the water as they quickly swam away. I stood there shaking with adrenaline and then trudged back slowly to the boat. My guide looked at me and said, "What happened to you out there?"

For the rest of the evening, I was the brunt of jokes about flailing in the water. As I kept reliving the sequence of events in my mind, I felt inept. I was awful. I had choked. I wasn't sure I'd be able to cast at all the next day. But as I halfheartedly began to get my gear together, it occurred to me: tomorrow is a fresh new day!

"It's not a simple matter for me to understand my fascination with fly-fishing. Is it the challenge of finding the one fly in my box that will entice a fish I see rising along a far bank? Is it the thrill of catching one of those beautiful fish, perhaps a cutthroat with brilliant colors showing that it only recently finished spawning? To touch it gently, to see its features up close, to watch its graceful movement as it swims away—all that comes from my fascination with living things."

—Jean Marlowe, age 58

My point is, *don't get discouraged.*

You can make your fishing experience what you want it to be. Sometimes I am rather fright-ful on the river, I think, because I get so intense about fly-fishing. At other times, though, I enjoy a very leisurely day, spending more time looking at clouds and birds than at fish. The great thing is that the experience can be intense and goal oriented—or not. Success can be measured any way you choose. You don't have to gauge it by the number or size of the fish you catch. Were you able to put the fly exactly where you wanted it that time? Were you able to cast several times before getting your line tangled? Did you achieve the perfect drift or presentation? Relax, enjoy it. After all, this is supposed to be fun, right? I always tell people that if I had stayed with fly-fish-ing strictly because of how many fish I caught when I was getting started, I would have given it up years ago!

Chapter 10

RECOMMENDED BOOKS

Aquatic Entomology

Pobst, Dick. *Trout Stream Insects: An Orvis Streamside Guide.* New York: Lyons & Burford, 1990.

Schollmeyer, Jim. *Hatch Guide for Lakes: Naturals and Their Imitations for Stillwater Trout Fishing.* Portland OR: Frank Amato Publications, 1995.

Schollmeyer, Jim. *Hatch Guide for Western Streams.* Portland OR: Frank Amato Publications, 1997.

Whitlock, Dave. *Dave Whitlock's Guide to Aquatic Trout Foods.* Tulsa OK: Winchester Press, 1982.

Casting

Kreh, Lefty. *Longer Fly Casting.* New York: Lyons & Burford, 1991.

Krieger, Mel. *The Essence of Flycasting.* San Francisco: Club Pacific, 1987.

Wulff, Joan Salvato. *Joan Wulff's Fly Casting Accuracy.* New York: Lyons Press, 1997.

Wulff, Joan Salvato. *Joan Wulff's Fly-Casting Techniques.* New York: N. Lyons, 1987.

Destinations

Bartholomew, Marty. *Flyfisher's Guide to Colorado.* Gallatin Gateway MT: Wilderness Adventures Press, 1998. (Books in the Flyfisher's Guide to series are also available for Idaho, Montana, Northern California, Northern New England, and Wyoming.)

Graham, Yvonne, ed. *A Woman's No Nonsense Guide to Fly Fishing Favorite Waters,* Sisters OR: David Communications, 2000.

Fly-Fishing Strategy

Brown, Dick. *Fly Fishing for Bonefish*. New York: Lyons & Burford, 1993.

Hughes, Dave. *Reading the Water: A Fly Fisher's Handbook for Finding Trout in All Types of Water*. Harrisburg PA: Stackpole Books, 1988.

Kreh, Lefty. *Flyfishing in Salt Water*. New York: Lyons Press, 1997.

Livingston, A. D. *Bass on the Fly*. Camden ME: Ragged Mountain Press, 1994.

Reynolds, Barry, Brad Befus, and John Berryman. *Carp on the Fly: A Flyfishing Guide*. Boulder CO: Johnson Books, 1997.

Reynolds, Barry, and John Berryman. *Beyond Trout: A Flyfishing Guide*. Boulder CO: Johnson Books, currently out of print.

Reynolds, Barry, and John Berryman. *Pike on the Fly: The Flyfishing Guide to Northerns, Tigers, and Muskies*. Boulder CO: Johnson Books, 1993.

Rickards, Denny. *Fly-Fishing Stillwaters for Trophy Trout*. Stillwater Productions, 1998.

Streeks, Neale. *Drift Boat Fly Fishing: A River Guide's Sage Advice*. Portland OR: Frank Amato Publications, 1995.

Fly-Tying

Morris, Skip. *Art of Tying the Bass Fly: Flies for Largemouth Bass, Smallmouth Bass, and Pan Fish*. Portland OR: Frank Amato Publications, 1996.

Morris, Skip. *Fly Tying Made Clear and Simple*. Portland OR: Frank Amato Publications, 1992.

Van Vliet, John. *The Art of Fly Tying*. Minnetonka MN: Cowles Creative Publishing, 1998.

Knots

Sherry, J. E. *The Fisherman's Ultimate Knot Guide* (pocket card).

Traux, Doug. *Orvis Waterproof Vest Pocket Knot Booklet*.

Fly-Fishing with Children

Brunquell, Philip, M.D. *Fly-Fishing with Children: A Guide for Parents*. Woodstock VT: Countryman Press, 1994.

Women's Experiences

Foggia, Lyla. *Reel Women: The World of Women Who Fish*. Hillsboro OR: Beyond Words, 1995.

Morris, Holly, ed. *A Different Angle: Fly Fishing Stories by Women*. New York: Seal Press, 1995.

Morris, Holly, ed. *Uncommon Waters: Women Write about Fishing*. Seattle: Seal Press, 1991.

Page, Margot. *Little Rivers: Tales of a Woman Angler*. New York: Lyons & Burford, 1995.

MAGAZINES

American Angler
P.O. Box 4100
Bennington VT 05201-4100
802-447-1518
fax 802-447-2471
http://www.flyfishmags.com

Fly Fisherman
P.O. Box 8200
6405 Flank Dr.
Harrisburg PA 17105-8200
717-657-9555
Fax 717-657-9526

Fly Fishing in Salt Waters
2001 Western Ave., Suite 210
Seattle WA 98121
206-443-3273
Fax 206-443-3293
http://www.flyfishinsalt.com

Fly Rod & Reel
P.O. Box 370
Camden ME 04843
207-594-9544
Fax 207-594-5144
E-mail: jbutler@flyrodreel.com

Fly Tyer
P.O. Box 4100
Bennington VT 05201-4100
802-447-1518
Fax 802-447-2471
http://www.flyfishmags.com

Warmwater Fly Fishing
P.O. Box 4100
Bennington VT 05201-4100
802-447-1518
Fax 802-447-2471
http://www.flyfishmags.com

Wild Steelhead & Salmon
4105 East Madison St., Suite 2
Seattle WA 98112
206-328-5760
Fax 206-328-8761
E-mail: salmon@
    wildsteelhead.com
subscriptions: P.O. Box 3666,
Seattle WA 98124

DIRECTORIES

Black's Fly Fishing
P.O. Box 2029
Red Bank NJ 07701
732-224-8700
800-722-2677
Fax 800-552-3910
This annual contains information
about fly-fishing schools, guide
services, lodges, equipment manufacturers, tackle dealers, fly-fishing
shows, and expos state by state.
E-mail: blacksporting@msn.com

Masters Press
2647 Waterfront Pkwy. E Dr.
Suite 300
Indianapolis IN 46214
800-722-2677
Fax 800-552-3910

*Orvis Endorsed Guides and
Lodges* (see list in Orvis Fishing
and Outdoor Catalog)

GEAR

Cabela's
1 Cabela Dr.
Sidney NE 69160
800-237-4444
308-234-5555
http://www.cabelas.com

Cortland Line Company
P.O. Box 5588
3736 Kellogg Rd.
Cortland NY 13045
607-756-2851
http://www.cortlandline.com

Damselfly
P.O. Box 440
Moyie Springs ID 83845
800-966-4166
Fax 208-267-9316
http://www.outdoorswoman.com

Farrows
13509 E. Boundary Rd., Suite E
Midlothian VA 23112
804-744-9359
888-467-2779
E-mail: sassy@sassysara.com
http://www.farrows.com

G. Loomis (rods)
1359 Down River Dr.
Woodland WA 98674
800-662-8818
http://www.gloomis.com

L.L. Bean
Casco St.
Freeport ME 04033
800-809-7057
http://www.llbean.com

Orvis Company
1711 Blue Hills Dr.
Roanoke VA 24012
800-548-9548
http://www.orvis.com

Outdoor Woman
P.O. Box 7603
Boise ID 83707
208-385-9606
888-565-0907
http://www.theoutdoorwoman.
    com

Sage Manufacturing
8500 NE Day Rd.
Bainbridge Island WA 98110
800-533-3004
E-mail: Sage@SAGEflyfish.com
http://www.SAGEflyfish.com

R. L. Winston Rod Company
P.O. Box 411
500 South Main St.
Twin Bridges MT 59754
800-237-7763
406-684-5674
http://www.winstonrods.com

ORGANIZATIONS

Becoming an OutdoorsWoman
Diane Lueck/Christine Thomas
College of Natural Resources
University of Wisconsin–
Stevens Point
Stevens Point WI 54481
715-228-2070
http://www.uwsp.edu/bow

Colorado Women Flyfishers
Kris Tita
P.O. Box 46035
Denver, CO 80201
http://www.colowomenflyfishers.org

Federation of Fly Fishers
502 S. 19th, Suite 1
P.O. Box 1595
Bozeman MT 59771-1595
406-585-7592
E-mail: 74504.2605@
    compuserve.com
http://www.fedflyfishers.org

International Women Fly Fishers
c/o Baja on the Fly
Yvonne Graham
P.O. Box 81961
San Diego CA 92138
800-919-2252
Fax 619-223-0221
E-mail: bajafly@aol.com
http://www.bajafly.com

Trout Unlimited
1500 Wilson Blvd., Suite #310
Arlington VA 22209-2310
703-522-0200

WOMEN'S FLY-FISHING CLASSES

Blue Quill Angler
Dana Rikimaru
1532 Bergen Pkwy.
Evergreen CO 80439
800-435-5353
http://bluequillangler.com
E-mail: dana@
bluequillangler.com

L.L. Bean Fly-Fishing School
Outdoor Discovery Schools
Freeport ME 04033
888-552-3261
http://www.llbean.com/odp

Orvis Fly-Fishing Schools
Orvis Company
1711 Blue Hills Dr.
Roanoke VA 24012
800-235-9763

Reel Women Outfitters, Inc.
Lori-Ann Murphy
P.O. Box 289
Victor ID 83455
208-787-2657
E-mail: info@reel-women.com
http://www.reel-women.com

GUIDED FISHING FLOAT TRIPS

ArkAnglers
Greg Felt and Rod Patch

7500 West Hwy 50
Salida CO 81201
719-539-4223
http://www.canyonmarine.com

Reel Women Outfitters, Inc.
See contact information, left.

Index

Numbers in **bold** refer to pages with illustrations

A

Adams, 76, 113, 141, 143
Adams Parachute, 113
Albright knot, **65**, 100
altitude sickness, 24, 127
Anthony, Jill, 19, 40
arbor knot, **64**
ArkAnglers, 133
Armour, Bessie, 30

B

back cast, 49, **50**
  and false casting, 60
  in a float tube, 133
  troubleshooting, 55, 56
backing, 63, **64**, 100
Baetis Nymph, 141
bandannas, 114
Barry, Gracia, 17
Bartholomew, Marty, 43
bass, 26, 41, 42, 93, 100
Bead-Head Caddis Larva, 142
Becoming an Outdoors Woman,
  130, 149
belly boats, **132–33.** See also float
  tubes
Black Gnat, **37**
Blood Midge, 142
bluegill, 26, 41, 42
Blue Wing Olive, 141
Blue Wing Olive Wet, 113
boats, 24, 29, 42
bonefish, 130, 145
books, 147–48
Brassie, 142
Brunquell, Philip, 136, 148
Buckskin, 142
butt cap, **31**

C

butt section (of rod), **31**, **32**, 63,
  65
butt section (of line), 35, 65, 70

caddis flies, 140, 141–42
Cannon's Suspender Midge, 142
canoeing, 42, 131
Canyon Marine Whitewater Expeditions, 133
carp, 42
casting, 31, **55**
  advanced, 57–60, **58**, **61**, 62
  back cast, 49, **50**
  closed wrist, **56**
  false, 59–60
  forward cast, 49, **51–54**, **55**
  from a float tube, 132–33
  grip, **49**
  learning, 46–47, 62
  lining the fish, 78, **79**
  mending the line, **80–81**, 82
  motion of, 49–54
  open wrist, **56**
  practicing, 47–**56**, 57
  problems with, 54–57, **56**
  putting the fish down, 78
  quartering upstream, 78–**79**
  right-handed or left-handed,
    33–34
  rod loading, 50
  roll cast, **61**, 62
  in spin-fishing, 46
  stance, 48–49
  stripping in the slack, 83
  theory, 46
  tight and wide loops in, **51**, 54
  and women, 47
casting arm, 49
casting hand, 49
casting side, 48

D

catch. See playing the fish; strikes
catch-and-release, 18, 44, 78, **85**
  and classroom curriculum, 26
  how to, **88**, 117
  landing nets for, 115
  net bag for, 117
  reasons for, 28, 40, 86, 89–90
  regulations on, 89
checklists, 116
  emergency supplies, 125
  for vest pockets, 114
chest pack, **115**
children, and fly fishing, 134,
  135–36
classes, 25–26, 149–50
  for casting, 56
  for children, 136
  and expense, 29
  family, 29, 135–36
  in fly-tying, 144
clinch knot, **38**, **64**, 68, 71, 112
clothing, 102–5
  and color, 102
  layering, 102, 103
  worn under waders, 103, 105, 109
cold-water fish, 26
cold-water fishing, 41
Colorado Women Flyfishers
  (CWF), 130
Corkern, Gail, 17–18, 25
cover
  in moving water, 74
  in still water, 75
crappie, 41, 42
creeks, 29, 41, 93
CWF. See Colorado Women Fly-
  fishers

double overhand (surgeon's) knot,
  68, **70–71**

drag, 79
  remedy for, **80**–81
drift boat, **131**
drinking water, 127
dry flies, 29, **36**
  for beginners, 37–38, 113
  fishing with, 75, **76**–81, 139
  and fish rising, 76–77
  flotant for, 113
  insects imitated by, 138, 140,
    142–43
  parachute, **76**
  presentation of, 77, **78**–**80**, 81
  setup for, 77
  and terrestrials, 142, 143
  traditional, **76**

E
Elk Hair Caddis, **38**, 76, 113, 142
  recommended for beginners, 37, 40
emergency supplies, 124, 125
Emerger, 113
emergers, 81, 140, 141, 142
entomology, 25–26, 137
equipment. *See* gear

F
false casting, 59–60
fanny pack, 115
Federation of Fly Fishers (FFF), 129
ferrule, **31**
Felt, Greg, 133
FFF. *See* Federation of Fly Fishers
first-aid kit, 114, 125
fish
  diet of, 140–42
  dispatching of, 88
  feeding habits of, 15, 138
  freshwater, 93
  handling, 28–29, **88**
  landing, 78, **85**
  mucus coating of, 29, 88
  playing, 26, 78, 86
  releasing (*see* catch-and-release)
  restrictions on, 43–44
  saltwater, 93
  species of, and recommended rod
    weights and lengths, 93, 94,
    100
  strikes, 81

fishing license, 43–44, 114
fishing season, 44
Flashback Pheasant Tail, 45
flies, 62, 63. *See also* dry flies;
    emergers; nymphs; streamers;
    wet flies
  appearance of, 15, 29, 45–46
  for beginners, 37–38, 40, 113
  and classes in fly-fishing, 26
  costs of, 36
  hackle on, 36, 76
  insects imitated by, 140–142
  recommended, 143–44
  selecting, 142–44
  size of, 36, **46**, 67
  size of, and leader taper, 67
  tied in attractor patterns, 45
  tied in exacting patterns, **45**
  tying on, 38 *See also* knots
  types of, **36**
float trips, 130, 131–32, 150
float tubes, 24, 42, **132**–**33**
  and fly rod length, 93
  and physical challenges, 133
  and pregnancy, 134
flotant
  and dry fly fishing, 77, 113
  recommended for beginners, 40
  types of, 38, 111, **113**
fly boxes, 43, 64, **113**, 114
Flyfisher's Guide to Colorado
    (Bartholomew), 43, 147
fly-fishing, 15
  attraction of, 16–21, 24–25, 146
  beginning, 22, 28–29, 30, 37,
    130, 145
  characteristics necessary for,
    22–24
  further adventures in, 128–33
  solo or with companions, 24, 40
Fly Fishing with Children (Brun-
    quell), 136, 148
fly line. *See* line
fly rods. *See* rods, fly
fly shops. *See* shops, fly-fishing
fly tackle dealers, 91, 94, 95
fly-tying, 144–45
Foggia, Lyla, 18, 148
forceps, **39**, 40, **86**, 112
forward cast, 49, **51**–**55**

G
gear, 31–40, 63–68
  acquiring, 27–28
  carrying, 117
  choices in, 117–18
  and classes in fly-fishing, 25, 26
  designed for women, 27, 93–94, 104
  mail order sources for, 149
  recommended for beginners, 40
  renting, 27
Giant Black Stone Fly, 141
gloves, 105
Golden Stone Fly, 141
Grasshopper, 113
Gray Hackle Peacock, **37**
Griffith's Gnat, 142
grips (rod), **31**
  full wells, **27**
  half wells, 94
  modified cigars, 94
  reversed half wells, **27**
  on women's rods, 94
group trips, 128–29, 150
guides (rod), **31**
guides, fishing, 130–31

H
hackle, 36, 76
Halsey, Laurie, 18
Hare's Ear, 81, 113, 141
Hare's Ear Wet, 141
hatches, 77, 137–38
hats, 47, 48, 105, 116
hemostat. *See* forceps
Hill, Chris, 123, 132
hook keeper, **31**, 34, **35**
hooks
  barbed, **86**
  barbless, **86**–87
  parts of, **37**
  removing from the fish, 86
  and safety, 29, 48, **86**
  setting, 78, 82
  sizes of, **37**, 46
hypothermia, 102

I
IFWFF. *See* International Festival
    of Women Fly Fishers
indicators. *See* strike indicators

insect repellent, 116, 125
insects, aquatic, 31
  categories of, 140–42
  characteristics of, 138
  and classroom curriculum, 25–26
  hatching, 137–38
  imitating with flies, **138**
  life stages of, 140
  observing, 137, 138–39, 139–40
  and wet flies, 82
insects, terrestrial. *See* terrestrials
insects, water. *See* insects, aquatic
International Festival of Women
    Fly Fishers (IFWFF), 14, 129
International Women Fly Fishers
    (IWFF), 129, 149
Irresistible, **37**

J
Jacobs, Angie, 40

K
Kaufman's Stone, 141
kayaking, 131
knots
  Albright, **64**, 100
  arbor, **64**
  and classroom curriculum, 25
  clinch, **38**, **64**, 68, 71, 112
  double overhand, 68, **70**–71
  and flotant, 111
  learning, 63, 69
  loop-to-loop, **35**, **64**, 70
  moistening, 68–69
  perfection loop, 68, **69**–70
  surgeon's, **64**, 68, **70**–71
  testing, 71
  tightening, 69
  tools for, **39**, 112
  types of, 68, **69**–**70**, 71

L
La Fontaine Sparkle Pupa, 142
lakes, 29, 41–42
  and beginners, 37
  float tubes in, 132
  and fly rod length, 93
  line used on, 100–101
  reading, 74–75
landing nets. *See* nets, landing

lanyard, **115**
leader kits, **66**
leaders, 35, **36**, 63, **64**, 112
  breaking strength of, 35
  for casting practice, 48
  and dry fly fishing, 77
  knotless, 66
  knotted, 66
  length of, 67
  and moving-water fishing, 67
  recommended for beginners, 40
  size of, and fly size, 67
  and still-water fishing, 80, 67
  and streamer fishing, 83
  tapering, 66–67, 68
  types of, 65–66
Leadwing Coachman, 81, 113
Light Cahill, 141
line, 31, 63
  acquiring, 27, 28, 99
  butt section of, 35, 65, 70
  caring for, 99
  and casting, 46
  for casting practice, 48, **49**, 50
  colors of, 101
  double-taper, **99**, 100
  and false casting, 59
  floating versus sinking, 65,
      100–101
  recommended for beginners, 101
  sink tip, 65
  taper of, 99
  and walking with a fly rod, **57**
  weight, 100
  weight-forward, **99**
line hand, 49
  and shooting line, 57, **58**
line setup, 25, 63–64, **64**
lining the fish, 54

M
Madame X, 141
magazines, fly-fishing, 148–49
maps, 43
marlin, 100
Marlowe, Jean, 145
mayflies, 140, 141
McMahon, Shari, 135
midges, 140, 142
Mingo, Suzanne, 63

Miracle Nymph, 113, 142
moving water, 41, 133. *See also*
    rivers; still water; streams
Muddler Minnow, **83**, 113

N
nets, landing, 29, 86, 115, **117**
nymphs, 29, 76
  appearance of, **36**
  fishing with, 75, 81, 82–83
  insects imitated by, 38, 140, 142
  recommended for beginners, 113
  of the stone fly, 141
  strike indicators for, 113
  weights for, 113

O
Olive Woolly Bugger, 83
Orange Soft Hackle, **81**, 113, 141
organizations 129–30, 149
Orvis Fly-Fishing Schools, 26, 150
outfitters, 130–31, 149–50

P
pack rods, 92
Pale Morning Dun, 141
Palomino Midge, 142
panfish, 93, 100
Parento, Beth, 22
Peeking Caddis, 142
perfection loop (knot), **68**, 69–70
Perkins, Gwen, 129
Pheasant Tail, **81**, 113, 140, 141
physical challenges, 133–34
pike, 28, 42, 93
playing the fish, 26, 78
  give-and-take of, 86
ponds, 29, 41–42, 84
  and beginners, 37
  float tubes in, 132
  line used on, 101
  reading, 74
pontoon boats, **133**
pregnancy, 134
presentation, 15–16, 59. *See also*
    dry flies, presentation of
Prince Nymph, 81, 113, 141

R
rafting, 131

rain jacket, **103**, 104
Red and Black Ant, 113
reels, 25, 31, 40, 64
  arbor of, 63, **64**, **97**
  attaching, 32, 33–34
  backing on, 97
  buying, 27–28, 96, **97–98**
  cleaning and maintenance, 34, 96
  disc drag, **98**
  drag systems for, 98
  grit in, 34, 96
  large-arbor, **97**
  line guard on, **33**, 34
  parts of, **33**
  seats, **32**
  sizes of, and rod weights, 96–**97**
  spools on, 96–**97**
  spring-and-pawl drag, **98**
reel seats, **32**
Reel Women (Foggia), 18, 148
Reel Women Outfitters, 130, 150
regulations, 43–44
retractor. *See* zinger
Reynolds, Barry, 42, 136
Rio Grande King, 37
Rio Grande Trude, 37, **38**, 40, 113,
  140
rise forms, 41, 75, 76–77
rivers, 29, 41, 84
  casting in, 78–**79**
  cover in, 74
  float tubes in, 132
  leaders used on, 67
  line used on, 100–101
  nymph fishing in, 82, 83
  pools in, 41, **72**, 73, 101
  reading, 71–74, **72**
  riffles in, **72**, 73
  rod length for, 93
  runs in, **72–73**
  seams in, 73–74
  streamer fishing in, 83, 84
  transition zones in, 74
rod cases, 91
rods, fly
  assembling, 31–34, **32**
  bamboo, 94
  for beginners, 40
  borrowing, 27
  butt of, **31**, **32**, 63, 65

buying, 27–28, 91–96, **95**
for casting practice, 47, 48, 49
and classes in fly-fishing, 25, 26
designed for women, 93–94
disassembling, 33
fast-action, **95**
ferrule, **31**, 92
fiberglass, 94
flexes of, 94–**95**
full-flex, 94
graphite, 94
grips, **27**, **31**, 94
guides, **31**
hook keeper, **31**, 34, **35**
lengths of, 31, 93
materials used in, 94
medium-action, **95**
medium-flex, **95**
number of pieces of, 31, 93
parts of, **31**
recommended by fish species, 93,
  94
reel seat on, **31**, **32**
repairing, 96
for saltwater fly fishing, 27
slow-action rod, 94–**95**
soft, 94–**95**
stiff, **95**
stringing up, **34–35**
stripping guides, **31**, 34
tip flex, **95**
tip of, **31**, **32**
walking with, **57**
weights of, 31, 92, 93, 96–**97**,100
rod socks, 91
rod tubes, 91
roll cast, **61**, 62
Royal Trude, 37, 40, 113
Royal Wulff, 37, **38**, 40, 45, 113
RS2 Emerger, 141
running line, 99

S
safety, 28
  and chest waders, 106
  and classroom curriculum, 26
  and hooks, 29, 48
  and sunglasses, 39, 48
  and wading, 119–22, **121**
  and a wading belt, 107

as a woman, 122–25
salmon, 26, 89, 93
saltwater fly-fishing, 41, 42, 145
  care of gear in, 96
  classes for, 25, 26
  clothing for, 102, 105
  hooks for, 37
  rod weights and lengths for, 27,
    93, 100
  and streamers, 37, 84
schools, fly-fishing, 48, 149–50
seining, **139**
shark, 41, 100
shooting line, 57–59, **58**
shops, fly-fishing
  assistance with gear selection at,
    28, 91, 92, 93
  casting clinics offered by, 48
  classes taught in, 25, 136
  gear rented at, 27
  and guides, 131
  and places to fish, 43
  "Should Women Have Their Own
    Fly Rods?", 93–94
sight fishing, 74, 75
Smith, Glenda, 7, 16, 23
snips, **39**, 40, 112
socks, 105
Sofa Pillow, 141
Soft Hackle Orange, **81**, 113, 141
spin-fishing, 46, 96
Stalcup Bead-Head Caddis
    Emerger, 142
Steve's Stonefly, **37**
still water, 41. *See also* lakes;
    moving water; ponds
  dry-fly-fishing on, 80
  inlets and outlets in, 75
  leaders used on, 67, 80
  nymph fishing in, 83
  and pontoons, 133
  streamer fishing in, 84
Stimulator, 113, 141
Stocking Sedge, 142
stone flies, 140–41
stop (part of cast), 49, 50–51
streamers, 38, 75, 113
  appearance of, **36**, 143
  fishing with, 76, **83–84**
  for saltwater fly fishing, 37, 84

stream etiquette, 123–24, 125–26
streams, 37, 41. *See also* rivers
strike indicators
  jumping, 83
  for nymph fishing, 113
  types of, **82**, 112
strikes. *See also* playing the fish
  and tension on the line, 85–86
String Thing, 142
stripping line in, **58**
sunfish, 42
sunglasses, 39, 40, 47, 48, 114
sunscreen, 114, 125
surgeon's (double overhand) knot,
  64, 68, **70**–71
swimming, 28

T
tackle. *See* flies; gear; hooks; leaders;
    line; reels; rods, fly
Tan Elk Hair Caddis. *See* Elk Hair
    Caddis
tarpon, 93, 100
terrestrials, 113, 142, 143
Third Annual International Festival
    of Women Fly Fishers, 14, 129
Thompson, Martha Rodriguez, 134
tip section (of rod), **31**, **32**
tippet, 63, **64**, 68, 112
  and dry fly fishing, 77
  and practicing knot tying, 69, 70
toilet facilities, 126–27
transition zones
  in moving water, 74
  in still water, 75
Tronquet, Cathy, 17, 32
trout, 26
  rod weight for, 93, 100
  spawning, 89
  teeth of, 28, 86
Trout Unlimited (TU), 129, 136
tuna, 93, 100

V
vests, 110–12, **111**
  alternatives to, **115**
  designed for women, 104

loading, 112–14
worn by float tubers, 132

W
waders, 26, 27, 42, 102, 105–6
  bootfoot, **107**
  breathable, 103, 108–9
  chest, 106, **107**, 119–20
  clothing worn under, 103, 105,
    109
  designed for women, 104
  fit of, 109
  gravel guards for, **108**
  hippers, 106–**7**, 120
  materials used in, 108–9
  patching, 108
  in pontoon boats, 133
  and pregnancy, 134
  stockingfoot, **107**–8, 109
  wading belt over, **106**, 107, 120
  and wading boots, 109–**10**
  waist, 106
  worn by float tubers, 132
wading
  buddy system of, **121**
  and peer pressure, 119, 120, 121
  safety, 119–22
  wet wading, 106, 107
wading boots, 109–**10**
  ultralight, **110**
waist pack, **115**
walleye, 28
warm-water fishing, 26, 41
water
  access to, 24, 29
  drinking, 127
  locating, 43–44
  moving, 41, 71, **72**, 73–74
  reading, 31, 41, 71, **72**, 73–75,
    84–85
  reading moving, 71, **72**, 73–74
  reading still, 74–75
  and safety, 28
  still, 41–42, 74–75
  types of, 40–42
water insects. *See* insects, aquatic
water purifier, **127**

WD40 (midge pattern), 142
weapons, 125
weather, 22
weights, **81**
  for nymph fishing, 113
  soft-weight, 81
wet flies, 75
  appearance of, **36**
  for beginners, 113
  fishing with, **81**–82
  insects imitated by, 138, 140, 142
whistles, 114, 125
Wickes, Nancy, 20, 42
windbreaker, 103–4
windshirt, **103**
women fly fishers, 13–14
  and age, 18, 20
  backgrounds of, 18
  and casting, 47
  classes for, 25–26, 149–50
  comaraderie shared by, 14, 26
  fly rods designed for, 93–94
  gear designed for, 93–94, 104
  and men fly fishers, 13–14, 23, 26,
    122–23
  organizations for, 129–30, 149
  outdoor educational programs for,
    130, 150
  physical considerations of, 22,
    133–34
  and safety, 122–25
Woolly Buggers, 73, **83**, 113, 144

X
X Caddis, 142

Y
Yellow Bead-Head Stone Fly, 141
Yellow Humpy, 76, 113
Yellow Woolly Bugger, 113
Young, Kathy, 18–19

Z
zinger, **39**